A Leader's Guide to
The **Courage** to Be
YOURSELF

A Leader's Guide to
The **Courage** to Be
YOURSELF

Al Desetta, M.A., and Sherrie Gammage, M.Ed.,
with Educators for Social Responsibility

esr

EDUCATORS FOR SOCIAL RESPONSIBILITY

free spirit
PUBLiSHiNG®

Helping kids
help themselves™
since 1983

ISBN-13 978-1-57542-187-2

ISBN-10 1-57542-187-9

At the time of this book's publication, all facts and figures cited are the most current available; all telephone numbers, addresses, and Web site URLs are accurate and active; all publications, organizations, Web sites, and other resources exist as described in this book; and all have been verified. The authors and Free Spirit Publishing make no warranty or guarantee concerning the information and materials given out by organizations or content found at Web sites, and we are not responsible for any changes that occur after this book's publication. If you find an error or believe that a resource listed here is not as described, please contact Free Spirit Publishing. Parents, teachers, and other adults: We strongly urge you to monitor children's use of the Internet.

Edited by Eric Braun and Sarah Fazio
Cover and interior design by Marieka Heinlen

10 9 8 7 6 5 4 3 2 1
Printed in the United States of America

Free Spirit Publishing Inc.
217 Fifth Avenue North, Suite 200
Minneapolis, MN 55401-1299
(612) 338-2068
help4kids@freespirit.com
www.freespirit.com

As a member of the Green Press Initiative, Free Spirit Publishing is committed to the three Rs: Reduce, Reuse, Recycle. Whenever possible, we print our books on recycled paper containing a minimum of 30% post-consumer waste. At Free Spirit it's our goal to nurture not only children, but nature too!

green press INITIATIVE

Dedicated to young adults who have endured teasing, harassment, bullying, or exclusion, and to the adult allies who have helped them. May this guide serve as an inspiration and source of hope.

ACKNOWLEDGMENTS

A Leader's Guide to The Courage to Be Yourself is based on the work of Educators for Social Responsibility (ESR), the national organization that teaches young people creative and productive ways of resolving conflict. We are especially indebted to Carol Miller Lieber, author of *Conflict Resolution in the High School: 36 Lessons* (ESR, 1998), upon which *A Leader's Guide to The Courage to Be Yourself* draws heavily for its sessions, organization, and inspiration. Without her work, this book would not have been possible. Larry K. Brendtro's article, "Worse than Sticks and Stones: Lessons from Research on Ridicule," *ESR Forum,* provided a comprehensive overview of teasing and harassment among teens.

Jeff Perkins, former director of publications and marketing at ESR, was our editorial colleague throughout the conception and development of this guide. We thank him for his important contributions. Thanks to ESR consultant and writer Heather Coulehan who reviewed the manuscript. Thanks also to Larry Dieringer, executive director of ESR, and to Tom Roderick, executive director of ESR, Metropolitan, for their help with this project.

We owe a great deal of gratitude to Keith Hefner, founder and executive director of Youth Communication, for his generosity in making available the stories in *The Courage to Be Yourself,* which provide the foundation for the activities in this leader's guide. Youth Communication is a nationally recognized writing program for teens that publishes two award-winning magazines where the stories originally appeared—*New Youth Connections* and *Represent* (the latter written by youth in foster care). We are also greatly indebted to the Youth Communication editors who originally worked with the teen authors to craft their stories: Rachel Blustain, Andrea Estepa, Clarence Haynes, Kendra Hurley, Philip Kay, Nora McCarthy, and Tamar Rothenberg.

Finally, our thanks to Judy Galbraith, publisher and president of Free Spirit Publishing, and Margie Lisovskis, editorial director, for their support and guidance. And we are grateful to Eric Braun, editor, and Sarah Fazio, assistant editor, for strengthening this book with their adept and perceptive editing.

Contents

List of Reproducible Pages

Introduction:
Accepting Differences, Promoting Peace

"Teaching young people to manage their emotions, resolve conflict nonviolently, and respect differences is just as important as teaching reading and math."

—Linda Lantieri
Founding Director, Resolving Conflict Creatively Program

Cliques, conflicts, and peer pressure form a pervasive backdrop to social interaction in middle and high schools. When differences among teens escalate to teasing, harrassment, exclusion, and bullying, everyone in the school community is affected. Learning is interrupted, students feel unsafe and insecure, and a heavy emotional burden is carried by targets, aggressors, and witnesses alike. Yet the complexities of teen relationships are usually invisible to adults.

The following statistics paint a stark picture of the far-reaching effects of teen peer conflict.

▌ In 2001, the Kaiser Family Foundation conducted a survey of young people regarding "tough issues." Of the teens interviewed:

- 86 percent said students at their school are teased and bullied.

- 68 percent said students at their school are treated badly because they are different.

- 60 percent said students at their school are threatened with violence by other students.

- 54 percent said they never talk with a guidance counselor or teacher about what's going on in their lives.[1]

▌ Seven percent of all 8th-grade students in the United States stay home at least once each month from fear of being picked on. One estimate is that 160,000 kids stay home from school every day in the United States because of conflict with peers.[2]

▌ The World Health Organization and Health Canada polled students in grades 6–10. The students were asked about their experiences in the current school term and the results showed:

- 14 percent were threatened at school.

- 20 percent reported being hit, slapped, or pushed.

- 35 percent were bullied

- 39 percent admitted to bullying classmates at least once.[3]

▌ A survey showed that 31 percent of lesbian, gay, bisexual, and transgender (LGBT) students were either threatened with a weapon or injured with a weapon in the previous 12 months.[4]

▌ A nationwide sample of students in 8th–11th grades found that 81 percent of students—79 percent of boys and 83 percent

1

of girls—experience sexual harassment often, occasionally, or rarely (even rarely is too often). Of students who were sexually harassed:

- 16 percent stayed home from school at least once.
- 20 percent found it hard to pay attention in class.
- 24 percent reported speaking less in class.[5]

■ A study commissioned by the U.S. Secret Service and the U.S. Department of Justice found that many of the attackers in school shootings had been harassed or bullied. While myriad complicated factors have contributed to school shootings, teasing and harassment were key factors in many of them, and "could have been a predictor of the attack" according to the study.[6]

■ ■ ■

Clearly, for modern teens, the social scene is thorny to say the least. In such a culture, teaching young people to respect differences and resolve conflicts peacefully is vital.

Most books that address teen conflict discuss ways to prevent or resolve it without looking closely at *why* young people have conflicts in the first place. *A Leader's Guide to the Courage to Be Yourself* takes a different approach. The methods in this book were developed by Educators for Social Responsibility (ESR), one of the largest and longest-running school-based organizations in the United States for conflict resolution, violence prevention, and inter-group relations. Specifically, the sessions in this guide are adapted from Carol Miller Lieber's *Conflict Resolution in the High School: 36 Lessons* (ESR, 1998), whose lessons form a foundation for ESR's conflict resolution program in secondary schools. Applying Lieber's work to the 26 true stories by teens in *The Courage to Be Yourself,*

this leader's guide focuses on the root causes of teen conflict so they can be discussed, analyzed, and addressed by you and the young people you work with.

When Diversity Leads to Conflict

Young people often feel confused or threatened by peers who dress differently, come from a different racial or ethnic background, live in a different neighborhood, engage in non-stereotypical activities, or are different from themselves in some other way. Lack of understanding and respect for difference often leads teens to label and categorize one another. Forming like-minded groups or cliques—with membership determined by race, style of clothing, athletic prowess, or other outward traits—gives teens a sense of security and meets a need for connection and belonging. But such benefits are often gained at the expense of those who are excluded or banished from the group. When young people define themselves and others primarily by the groups to which they belong, they set the stage for emotional, psychological, or physical conflict with their peers.

Most conflict among teens takes the form of peer pressure, teasing, exclusion, bullying, or harassment. Research shows that verbal ridicule and harassment can be as devastating as physical abuse, because of the way they deeply demean and stigmatize individuals.[7] Teens are engaged in a kind of continuous psychological warfare, conducted out of sight and below the radar of most adults. Even if adults are aware of this psychological warfare, they see only a small fraction of it, and they often lack the skills and tools needed to address the problem in a developmentally appropriate manner.

The complex factors that fuel these tensions and conflicts are often related to aspects of teen culture known only to teens themselves. Teens see adults as out of touch and, as a result, most remain silent. And the conflict goes on.

You can break that silence. These sessions will help you teach teens specific techniques to address the attitudes and behaviors that lead to conflict. Preventing and resolving conflict involves teaching young people to value and respect difference and diversity. By helping teens build character and increase their social and emotional intelligence, the activities in this book teach and reinforce core social values of respect, tolerance, integrity, truth, and social responsibility.

Targets, Aggressors, and Witnesses

All teens in a school or other community play a role in peer conflict, consciously or not. These sessions will enable you to reach three main roles—targets, aggressors, and witnesses.

- Targets often feel helpless to prevent the abuse they suffer, and fear retaliation if they seek help. The sessions will help you to build their confidence and assertiveness, and teach them problem-solving skills.

- Aggressors may feel little or no empathy for their targets and may have learned their behavior from being bullied or abused. The sessions will help you work with teens who bully to build their social and emotional competence, so that they understand the impact of their behavior on themselves and others.

- The majority of teasing and harassment occurs in the presence of other youth. Witnesses have the power to change a bullying situation by becoming an ally to the target. Witnesses are often unaware of this power and don't realize the importance of their role. Teens tend to take their cues from how other witnesses react; their actions and attitudes can ameliorate or worsen a conflict. The sessions will help you to encourage positive intervention by witnesses, so they can be part of the solution.

Teaching teens conflict resolution skills can be a difficult and even daunting task. *A Leader's Guide to The Courage to Be Yourself* will help you build tolerance and respect among the young people you work with by opening discussion and examining attitudes about diversity. It will help you teach teens to not only resolve conflict, but prevent it.

1. "Talking with Kids About Tough Issues: A National Survey of Parents and Kids." Menlo Park, CA: Kaiser Family Foundation and Children Now, 2001.
2. Olweus, Dan. *Bullying at School: What We Know and What We Can Do.* Malden, MA: Blackwell Publishers, 1993.
3. "Health Behavior in School-Aged Children: A World Health Organization Cross-National Study for Health Canada." Conducted by the Social Program Evaluation Group at Queens University at Kinston, 1998.
4. "Bullying in Schools: Harassment Puts Gay Youth at Risk." Alexandria, VA: National Mental Health Association, 2002.
5. "Hostile Hallways: Bullying, Teasing, and Sexual Harassment in School." Washington, DC: American Association of University Women Educational Foundation, 2001.
6. Fein, Ph.D., Robert A., Bryan Vossekuil, William S. Pollack, Ph.D., Randy Borum, Psy.D., William Modzeleski, and Marisa Reddy, Ph.D. *Threat Assessment in Schools: A Guide to Managing Threatening Situations and to Creating Safe School Climates.* Washington, DC: U.S. Secret Service and U.S. Department of Education, 2002.
7. Brendtro, Ph.D., Larry K., "Worse than Sticks and Stones: Lessons from Research on Ridicule," *ESR Forum* 18:2 (2001), pp. 1, 5, 9. Hoover, John H., and Ronald Oliver, *The Bullying Prevention Handbook: A Guide for Principals, Teachers, and Counselors.* Bloomington, IN: National Educational Service, 1996.

Leading the Sessions

This leader's guide is designed to be used with the anthology, *The Courage to Be Yourself: True Stories by Teens About Cliques, Conflicts, and Overcoming Peer Pressure.* Each of the 26 sessions in the leader's guide is based on a true story from the anthology and the themes it addresses. The sessions can be used in a variety of settings—regular classrooms, elective classes, advisory or family groups, after-school groups, service learning and leadership programs, and community- or faith-based settings. They can be conducted by both novice and experienced leaders who work with teens, including teachers, youth group leaders, counselors, clinicians, diversity coordinators, prevention specialists, and social workers.

The goals of the sessions are to teach teens to resist labeling and stereotyping their peers, to value and respect difference and diversity, and to resolve conflict peacefully when it arises. The stories in the anthology engage young people by reflecting their own experiences and modeling varied forms of positive behavior—the writers overcome stereotypes and preconceptions, befriend peers who are "different," resist peer pressure and conformity, and learn to better manage difficult emotions. The sessions explain how to use the stories to facilitate discussion and reflection on the larger themes. They use a combination of reading, writing, discussion, and experiential group activities to help teens deepen their understanding of the roots of conflict and how it might be prevented.

The sessions are designed to take approximately 50–55 minutes, but that time may vary depending on the size of your group, the setting in which you are leading the sessions, and the amount of time you wish to spend focusing on a particular activity. In many of the sessions, we provide suggestions for additional activities to extend the session beyond that time period, or to continue it on a different day.

The activities take a highly interactive approach that challenges young people to define, explore, defend, and change their attitudes and beliefs. Using time-tested teaching strategies, these activities will help teens to:

- define stereotyping, prejudice, and discrimination

- understand why labels and stereotypes are harmful

- uncover their own preconceptions and stereotypes

- understand their feelings and learn to express them in healthy ways

- respect and appreciate diversity and difference

- learn critical thinking and conflict-prevention skills

- identify strategies for resolving conflict

- contribute to improving the school or community culture

The sessions have three primary goals:

1. **To define the problem.** By reading the stories and participating in activities related to them, teens will learn to recognize teasing, harassment, and other forms of conflict, understand why conflict happens, and become more aware of why it's a problem.

2. **To prevent conflicts.** The sessions focus on activities that build understanding and empathy and help teens examine their attitudes toward diversity and

difference, find common ground, and work cooperatively.

3. To urge teens to intervene in conflicts.
The sessions feature activities that will:

- give targets specific, tangible skills they can use when they encounter peer pressure or harassment

- teach witnesses how to intervene effectively if they see an incident taking place

- teach group members specific techniques like anger management, peer mediation, and conflict resolution that can be used to settle disputes among their peers

HOW THE SESSIONS WORK

The sessions are designed to be easy to follow and easy to adapt. They offer specific guidelines for working with the stories in *The Courage to Be Yourself,* but because you have your own teaching style and strengths, you should feel free to lead group sessions in ways that suit you and meet the needs of the teens you're working with. You can modify sessions to make them shorter or longer, to focus on particular parts of the stories, or to connect them to other subjects you are covering.

Each session plan contains an Overview and a Session. In addition, many sessions have reproducible handouts that you may copy and distribute to your group.

Overview

The Overview is a reference for you and is not presented to the group. It provides an at-a-glance summary of the story and session. The Story Summary describes the assigned reading in two to three sentences and may be written on the board during the session. (You will also

ask volunteers to summarize the story in their own words, and the summary provided in the session plan can be used as a companion or comparison.)

The list of Materials highlights the reproducible handouts and anything else you'll need to complete the session's activities. Ideally, group members should bring their copies of *The Courage to Be Yourself* to each session. Under Prep Work you'll find a description of the preparation you'll need to do before your group meets for that session, such as writing the agenda on the board, making handouts, and setting up the room. The Objectives for each session focus on the skills or consciousness-raising themes group members will work toward. Themes for each session summarize subject matter that will be covered. Links to the Academic Curriculum will help you draw connections between session activities, classroom skills, and academic content.

The Session

The Session is what you present to the group and work through with them. Each session has four parts: a Preview, Gathering, Activity, and Closing.

Preview. The leader briefly goes over the agenda (which she or he has put on the board or flip chart before the meeting), highlighting the subject matter and objectives for the day.

Gathering. A brief activity brings the group's focus to the day's themes and helps prepare the group for the main activities that follow. This activity sets the stage for learning and is designed to hook the group members.

Activity. The main part of the session, the activity—or activities—is based on a story from *The Courage to Be Yourself* and is designed to help you achieve the session's goals. The activities ask teens to relate their personal experiences to the experiences of the story's writer.

Closing. End the session on a positive note. The closing is a brief activity related to the main themes or objectives of the session and can help you check the group's understanding of the main points covered in the session.

The Preview, Gathering, Activities, and Closing create a comprehensive session that will challenge the group—as well as the individual—to grow. Participating in all four parts will help teens personally engage with the content of the stories and is more likely to facilitate behavioral change compared to a more cognitive lesson. However, if you don't have 50–55 minutes to devote to a full session, or if you prefer to focus on the more academic main activities, you may skip the Preview, Gathering, and Closing.

SELECTING AND ORGANIZING THE SESSIONS

All 26 sessions in *A Leader's Guide to The Courage to Be Yourself* are self-contained and can stand alone. You may choose to conduct only a few sessions with your group of teens. Even a single session can help raise teens' acceptance and appreciation of diversity. However, the guide's positive lessons are much more powerful when they are reinforced through a program of several sessions.

You may choose to present the sessions to your group in the order they appear in this book, which matches the order of the stories in *The Courage to Be Yourself,* or you may choose to select sessions and present them in an order that suits your needs more specifically. To help you select and organize sessions, we offer two methods of grouping the sessions: by subjects and themes, and by the stages involved in conflict.

Subjects and Themes

Following is an index of major subjects and themes the sessions and stories cover. Using this index, you can choose and organize sessions to fit your goals as a leader and the needs of your group. For example, you may use this index of subjects and themes to find sessions that match up with other material you are teaching, or you may use it to create a themed unit that focuses on a single topic, such as anger or peer pressure. You may also choose sessions covering a variety of themes to teach a broader unit on conflict.

Anger

Session 16: Understanding Power—Who Has It? Who Doesn't? Beating the Bullies

Session 17: Exploring the Nature of Conflict, It Ain't Easy Being Hard

Session 20: All About Anger, My Group Home Scapegoat

Teasing, Bullying, and Harassment

Session 1: We All Belong to Groups (Part 1), In Defense of Misfits

Session 3: What Is Harassment? Afraid to Learn

Session 4: How Do We Experience Conflict? Sticking with Your "Own Kind"

Session 5: We All Belong to Groups (Part 2), Which Crowd Did You Pick?

Session 6: Acceptance in Your Life, Fashion Un-Conscious

Session 7: Interrupting Bullying and Harassment, Lighten Up on Heavy People

Session 8: Types of Peer Pressure, Losing My Friends to Weed

Session 9: Responding to Conflict—What Do We Do? (Part 1), Getting Guys off My Back

Session 11: Resisting Conformity, Princess Oreo Speaks Out

Racial and Ethnic Identity

Session 2: Being Different, A Stranger in a Strange School

Session 4: How Do We Experience Conflict? Sticking with Your "Own Kind"

Session 11: Resisting Conformity, Princess Oreo Speaks Out

Session 12: Interrupting Prejudice and Stopping Verbal Abuse, I'm Both Arab and American

Session 15: Racial and Ethnic Identity, Sticks and Stones

Session 23: Overcoming Preconceptions and Stereotypes (Part 2), A Different Kind of Friend

Resisting Peer Pressure/Resisting Conformity

Session 2: Being Different, A Stranger in a Strange School

Session 4: How Do We Experience Conflict? Sticking with Your "Own Kind"

Session 6: Acceptance in Your Life, Fashion Un-Conscious

Session 8: Types of Peer Pressure, Losing My Friends to Weed

Session 11: Resisting Conformity, Princess Oreo Speaks Out

Session 14: The Power of Cliques, Nasty Girls

Session 19: Responding to Conflict—What Do We Do? (Part 2), My Secret Love

School Culture

Session 1: We All Belong to Groups (Part 1), In Defense of Misfits

Session 2: Being Different, A Stranger in a Strange School

Session 3: What Is Harassment? Afraid to Learn

Session 4: How Do We Experience Conflict? Sticking with Your "Own Kind"

Session 5: We All Belong to Groups (Part 2), Which Crowd Did You Pick?

Session 6: Acceptance in Your Life, Fashion Un-Conscious

Session 7: Interrupting Bullying and Harassment, Lighten Up on Heavy People

Session 9: Responding to Conflict—What Do We Do? (Part 1), Getting Guys off My Back

Session 14: The Power of Cliques, Nasty Girls

Session 21: From Being a Bystander to Taking a Stand, There Are 20 Sides to Every Story

Session 22: Letting Go of Labels (Part 1), Who's the Real "Problem Child"?

Session 25: Introduction to Mediation, Back Off: Peer Mediation Can Help

Session 26: How Can People Make a Difference? My School Is Like a Family

Sexual Harassment

Session 9: Responding to Conflict—What Do We Do? (Part 1), Getting Guys off My Back

Session 13: Exploring the Nature of Violence, Gay on the Block

Sexual Orientation

Session 10: Countering Stereotypes and Prejudice, My Boy Wanted a Boyfriend

Session 13: Exploring the Nature of Violence, Gay on the Block

Session 24: Letting Go of Labels (Part 2), She's Cool, She's Funny, She's Gay

Styles of Dealing with Conflict

Session 9: Responding to Conflict—What Do We Do? (Part 1), Getting Guys off My Back

Session 19: Responding to Conflict—What Do We Do? (Part 2), My Secret Love

Valuing and Respecting Diversity

The Conflict Stages: From Roots to Resolution

Often, when teens experience conflict, it follows a pattern that can be broken down into four main stages. The first stage is the root of conflict. It occurs when teens do not respect diversity—and perhaps even fear it. This lack of respect for differences leads to the second stage: categorizing, labeling, and the forming of cliques. When teens separate themselves from one another this way, they may come to feel that those who are different from them—those who are in a different category—are less important than themselves. This feeling naturally leads to the third stage: conflict itself, such as peer pressure, exclusion, teasing, and bullying.

Conflict resolution is the fourth stage, though it may not always occur. Our goal with this book is to increase the frequency that it does. More than that, we hope to build in teens an appreciation for diversity so that fewer conflicts will arise in the first place.

It's helpful for teens to examine each of these conflict stages in order to understand why conflicts arise and how they can resolve them, prevent them, and grow from them. Following is an index that shows which sessions focus on which stages. By choosing sessions from each of the four conflict process stages, you can create your own unit to examine the issue of conflict in a progressive fashion. To take it further, you can create a progressive conflict unit on a specific subject or theme by cross-referencing sessions you select here with the subjects and themes index on pages 6–9.

1. Being Different

These sessions focus on the roots of teen conflict—a lack of understanding and respect for diversity and differences. The sessions will help teens examine their attitudes toward peers who are different from them in any number of ways, such as coming from a different racial or ethnic background, having different tastes in music and dress, or refusing to conform to the mainstream.

Session 11: Resisting Conformity, Princess Oreo Speaks Out

Session 13: Exploring the Nature of Violence, Gay on the Block

2. Labeling, Categorizing, and Forming Cliques

When young people fail to understand and respect diversity, they tend to label and categorize one another. These sessions explore why teens form cliques and label one another, and how those attitudes affect relationships between young people.

Session 5: We All Belong to Groups (Part 2), Which Crowd Did You Pick?

Session 14: The Power of Cliques, Nasty Girls

Session 18: Overcoming Preconceptions and Stereotypes (Part 1), At Home in the Projects

Session 19: Responding to Conflict—What Do We Do? (Part 2), My Secret Love

Session 22: Letting Go of Labels (Part 1), Who's the Real "Problem Child"?

3. Experiencing Conflict

When young people define themselves and others primarily by the groups they belong to, conflict often results. These sessions explore conflict in the forms it most often takes: teasing, exclusion, peer pressure, and bullying.

Session 3: What Is Harassment? Afraid to Learn

Session 6: Acceptance in Your Life, Fashion Un-Conscious

Session 7: Interrupting Bullying and Harassment, Lighten Up on Heavy People

Session 8: Types of Peer Pressure, Losing My Friends to Weed

Session 9: Responding to Conflict—What Do We Do? (Part 1), Getting Guys off My Back

Session 13: Exploring the Nature of Violence, Gay on the Block

Session 15: Racial and Ethnic Identity, Sticks and Stones

Session 16: Understanding Power—Who Has It? Who Doesn't? Beating the Bullies

Session 17: Exploring the Nature of Conflict, It Ain't Easy Being Hard

Session 20: All About Anger, My Group Home Scapegoat

4. Resolving Conflict and Respecting Diversity

These sessions teach teens ways to resist labeling and stereotyping; to value, respect, and celebrate differences and diversity; and to resolve conflict peacefully when it arises.

Session 10: Countering Stereotypes and Prejudice, My Boy Wanted a Boyfriend

Session 12: Interrupting Prejudice and Stopping Verbal Abuse, I'm Both Arab and American

Session 21: From Being a Bystander to Taking a Stand, There Are 20 Sides to Every Story

Session 23: Overcoming Preconceptions and Stereotypes (Part 2), A Different Kind of Friend

Session 24: Letting Go of Labels (Part 2), She's Cool, She's Funny, She's Gay

Session 25: Introduction to Mediation, Back Off: Peer Mediation Can Help

Session 26: How Can People Make a Difference? My School Is Like a Family

Preparing to Lead the Sessions

Before your group meets for the first time, you can prepare to lead *The Courage to Be Yourself* sessions by doing the following:

- Read *The Courage to Be Yourself* and the leader's guide, familiarizing yourself with the contents and themes of the stories and the teaching strategies and activities in the sessions. You may also want to consult other materials listed in the resources section on pages 137–142 of the leader's guide. Also, before leading any particular session, re-read that story and session before your group meets to make sure you understand the activities and themes and do any prep work necessary.

- If possible, make sure each group member has a copy of *The Courage to Be Yourself.*

- Review the teaching and learning strategies that are unfamiliar to you. A complete description of all the strategies used in this book can be found on pages 133–136.

- During the course of reading the stories and participating in the activities, some group members may reveal information that is highly sensitive or personal. Talk to your principal or your organization's director to make sure you understand your school's or organization's policies about discussing such issues. If a teen reveals that he or she is living in an abusive situation, you will likely have an obligation to report what you've heard. Regulations governing the reporting of child abuse differ from state to state. Many states have specific guidelines identifying certain professionals as "mandatory reporters." Check with your principal or director to determine the proper course of action and your responsibilities if such a situation should arise.

- Familiarize yourself with the school and community resources available to help young people deal with their problems. These can include school personnel, mental health agencies, shelters for homeless or abused young people, government agencies, and others.

- You may want to modify some activities to make them more appropriate for your group. For example, some stories and sessions (such as Session 10: Countering Stereotypes and Prejudice, which deals with LGBT stereotypes) are more appropriate for older, more mature teens. You know the needs of your group, so don't hesitate to make the modifications you feel are necessary before your group meets.

- Reflect on your own personal experiences with conflict. If you feel comfortable doing so, sharing these experiences with your group can be a powerful teaching tool and may encourage them to open up about their own lives.

As you continue conducting sessions with your class or group, keep the lines of communication open with a counselor, social worker, or psychologist at your school or in your community. Offer to share the content of your sessions with her or him, and discuss how to handle sensitive information revealed during group discussions or in group members' journals.

If you'd like group members to give you feedback about the sessions after your program is finished, in order to improve your program in the future, use the Group Assessment Questionnaire on page 130.

Getting Started

As your group's first meeting begins, welcome group members and introduce yourself. If there's room, have the group sit in a circle. Ask all of the teens to introduce themselves. You may ask them to share something about themselves they'd like the group to know.

Then, introduce the purpose of the group:

This group will be discussing and working with stories from a book called The Courage to Be Yourself. These true stories were written by teens about conflicts—such as peer pressure, teasing, bullying, and harassment—they've had with their peers. All of the writers used the conflict they wrote about as an opportunity to grow and find the courage to be themselves. We'll talk about the stories, do some group activities that will help us understand them better, and write about ways the stories connect with our own lives, feelings, and experiences.

Talk with your group about logistics. Make sure they know:

- where and when you'll be meeting
- what materials they should bring—paper and pen, a journal, and a copy of *The Courage to Be Yourself* (let them know if you're not providing the book for them)
- that they'll be expected to have read each session's story before the group meets for that session
- what to do if they miss a session

Next, talk about the importance of establishing and maintaining a positive and safe climate for your group. You won't have a productive session if group members don't feel comfortable opening up.

To begin establishing a positive and safe group climate, conduct the following activity for creating group guidelines. By involving group members in creating their own guidelines, you encourage healthy behavior and participation. The group feels ownership over the rules, which will increase their commitment to respecting and keeping them. (If you have already established guidelines with your group, skip the activity and simply review the guidelines and discuss possible additions or changes.)

ESTABLISHING A SAFE, RESPECTFUL, AND PRODUCTIVE ATMOSPHERE

To begin, ask group members to brainstorm a list of ideas that will help make the sessions a positive learning experience and a safe space to share their thoughts and feelings. What guidelines will help the group to work together productively? To communicate effectively and treat each other respectfully? Write the group's suggestions on the board or flip chart. If group members need help getting started, write down two or three guidelines, such as:

- Disagree with ideas, not people.
- Listen respectfully while other people share ideas—no rolling eyes or heaving sighs, just listening.

Whatever guidelines you and the teens establish, be sure to make the following non-negotiable policies clear:

- Everyone has the right to privacy. Even though many activities ask group members to share personal experiences, no one is required to share unless he or she is comfortable doing so. No one will be forced to say or do anything that makes him or her uncomfortable. If group members do share personal experiences, they should only share what they feel comfortable with others knowing. Tell the group that at times they will be writing in journals and their writing will not be shared publicly, unless they wish to share an entry with the group. Since journals won't be read by anyone (or perhaps only by you, if you require the group to turn in journals), teens should be encouraged to be honest in their writing. Honest self-reflection will provide them with the most benefit.

- Everyone has the right to confidentiality. Things that group members share in the course of discussions should stay in the room. However, members should also be aware that guaranteeing confidentiality in a group or school setting is not always possible.

- Everyone has the right to be treated with respect, which means no laughing at serious statements or personal stories, and no putting people down.

You may also wish to suggest the following guidelines for speaking and listening:

- Only one person speaks at a time.
- Give speakers your full attention and listen with an open mind.
- Don't interrupt someone who is speaking.
- Stay with the topic of discussion.
- Listen and discover rather than give advice or judge what others say.
- Be open and honest.
- Look at people when you speak to them.
- Disagree with ideas, not people.
- Say "I" when speaking for yourself.

After you've finished your list, discuss each item on the list with the group and make sure everyone understands each suggestion. Ask: *Have you ever been in situations where this suggestion was not observed? How would observing the suggestion make a difference in our group?*

After discussing the suggestions, ask for any revisions or objections to items on the list. When there are no more objections, have group members sign or initial the guidelines as an acknowledgment of their agreement to uphold them (if the guidelines are on flip chart paper; if they're on the board, type them up after the meeting and have the group sign them at your next meeting). If possible, post the guidelines in the room where you meet.

Revisiting the Guidelines

As you continue to meet, regularly revisit the guidelines with your group. Ask the group members:

- *Are the guidelines working?*
- *Does everyone feel safe, respectful, and productive?*
- *Are there additions or changes we should make?*

When you've finished establishing the guidelines, distribute copies of the anthology and assign the reading for your first session. Direct the group's attention to the Think About It questions following the story. Suggest that each person reflect on, and perhaps even write down some reactions to, these questions before the session.

We'd Like to Hear From You

We'd like to know how these stories and activities work for you. Write to us by mail or email.

Al Desetta, M.A.
Sherrie Gammage, M.Ed.
c/o Free Spirit Publishing Inc.
217 Fifth Avenue North, Suite 200
Minneapolis, MN 55401-1299
help4kids@freespirit.com

The Sessions

We All Belong to Groups (Part 1)

In Defense of Misfits, by Andrea Uva

Pages 7–11 in *The Courage to Be Yourself*

overview

Story Summary

Andrea attends a high school where cliques deeply divide the students. She feels rejected by the popular students, and joins a group of outsiders who hang out behind the school. While she deplores violence, she comes to understand how social exclusion infuriates young people and leads to conflict.

Materials

- Handout: Groups I Belong To
- Journals (optional)

Prep Work

- Make a copy of the Groups I Belong To handout (pages 21–22) for everyone in the group. Fill out your own copy.

- Optional: Write the following definition on the board or flip chart: "Culture: the beliefs, values, traditions, rituals, celebrations, and spiritual or religious practices that a group of people holds or does."

- Put the session's agenda on the board or flip chart (see Preview).

Objectives

Group members will:
- identify the groups they belong to by birth, by culture, and by choice
- share their thoughts and feelings about belonging to these groups

Themes

- Affirmation and acceptance
- Appreciation for diversity
- Personal connections
- Building community

Links to the Academic Curriculum

- Reading
- Reading comprehension
- Writing
- Public speaking

THE SESSION

Preview

Preview the agenda by telling the group that today you will discuss differences among people, the groups people belong to, and how these differences and groups can lead to stereotypes and conflicts. To do this, you will engage in the activities on this agenda:

Agenda: We All Belong to Groups

Reading: "In Defense of Misfits"
Gathering: Inside and Outside
Activity: Our Groups
- Summary
- Introduction
- Handout
- Large group discussion
- Small group discussion
Closing: Checking Out What We've Learned

Gathering: Inside and Outside

Pick one group member to stand next to you and have everyone else form a large circle. The remaining group member is the outsider. (If space is limited, choose five to six group members to form the circle and one person to be the outsider. The remaining group members act as observers, noting any impressions they have of the group or the person on the outside of the circle.)

Explain everyone's roles. Tell the circle to try to keep the person outside the circle from getting inside. Tell the outsider to try to get inside. The outsider can do this by trying to go between people's legs, pleading with individuals in the circle, or trying to gently push through the circle. He or she may not jump over the group or do anything that would injure anyone.

Allow five to six attempts and then call time. Ask the outsider what it felt like to have been kept from entering the group. Ask those on the inside how it felt to keep the outsider out.

Have the group return to their seats and ask them how the concept of "inside and outside" applies in their lives.

Activity: Our Groups

1. **Summary.** Ask for volunteers to summarize "In Defense of Misfits" in two to three sentences. You may wish to write the story summary on the board or flip chart as a reminder for the group. You may copy the summary provided on page 17 or a summary the group comes up with.

2. **Introduction.** Present the following mini-lecture about groups people are born into, grow up in, or choose: *Everyone belongs to groups. People are born into some groups, such as their race or ethnicity.*

   Cultural groups, such as religion, the places people live, or the languages they speak, acquire their members based upon how and when a person was brought up. Examples of cultural groups include being Canadian, a Spanish speaker, or Lutheran. These groups can change—a person can move to a different country, learn to speak a different language, and change religion.

   People also belong to groups by choice rather than birth. A person might join a soccer team, play in a band, write for a school newspaper, or volunteer at a local charity. A person might also choose to change her or his hair or eye color.

   Make sure the group understands the differences between these groups:

- Those that people are born into and do not change.

- Those (cultural groups) that people may be born into and can change.

- Those that people are not born into but can choose to belong to.

3. **Handout.** Pass out copies of the Groups I Belong To handout to the group. Before asking group members to complete their handouts, share your own filled-out questionnaire with them to make sure they understand the handout. Answer any questions or clarify concerns. Then, ask each group member to complete the Groups I Belong To handout, making sure everyone fills in at least two descriptions in each of the group categories.

4. **Large group discussion.** Point out to teens that many people have mixed feelings about some of the groups they belong to. Certain characteristics of a group may make them proud. Other characteristics of the same group may make them uncomfortable or angry. Tell group members to think about whether they have mixed feelings about any of the groups they put on their handout. Ask for volunteers to discuss their mixed feelings.

5. **Small group discussion.** Divide teens into groups of three to share their handout responses with each other. Encourage them to ask open-ended questions of each other that help them learn more about groups with which they are unfamiliar. For example, "How did you decide to place yourself in the _____ cultural group?" "I don't know a lot about _____. What can you tell me about this group?"

    Remind group members that they can choose what they want to share and what they don't. Allow 15 to 20 minutes for this discussion.

Closing: Checking Out What We've Learned

1. **Discussion or journals.** Choose one of the following questions for discussion or five minutes of reflective journal writing. (See page 134 for a complete description of journaling.)

- How did this experience change your understanding of some groups? Complete the sentence, "Before this activity I didn't know that _____."

- Think about one of the groups you belong to. When were you first aware that you were a member of that group?

- Think of a cultural group you don't belong to, but one you have had some contact with. When were you first aware of this group? What do you remember hearing others say about this group? What was your first personal experience with someone from this group? Did your thoughts about this group change after coming to know an individual from this group? If so, in what ways?

- Sometimes we're uncomfortable with the assumptions and stereotypes associated with a group we belong to. What stereotypes and assumptions do you wish could disappear? Consider this example:

    "It is utterly exhausting being black in America. . . . While many minority groups and women feel similar stress, there is no respite or escape from your badge of color. . . . The constant burden to 'prove' that you are as smart, as honest, as interesting, as wide-gauging and motivated as any other individual tires you out. . . ."—Marian Wright Edelman, president of the Children's Defense Fund

- Sometimes our loyalty to a group conflicts with the feelings, values, and desires we experience as individuals. Discuss or write about a time when you had to make a choice between following the expected beliefs and attitudes of your group or following your own personal beliefs.

2. **Group wishes.** Ask each group member to think about a group that he or she belongs to, such as males or females, teenagers, families, or students at school.

Ask group members to consider how they might complete the following sentence: "I wish more (group name) would _____." To provide an example, you can use the following sentence about adults (or a similar one you come up with): ***I wish more adults would sit for 15 minutes each day and just listen to kids, without interrupting.***

Ask for several volunteers to share their sentences with the group.

Assign a story from *The Courage to Be Yourself* to be read for your group's next meeting.

GROUPS I BELONG TO

1. Identify two groups you belong to by birth (such as physical characteristics, physical gifts, gender, race, or ethnicity).

1. _____

2. _____

2. Identify four groups that reflect your cultural identity (groups you may be born into but can change, such as geographical region, religion, social and economic status, language spoken).

1. _____

2. _____

3. _____

4. _____

3. Identify three groups you belong to by choice (such as sports teams, clubs, youth groups, job, other interests).

1. _____

2. _____

3. _____

4. Describe one thing about yourself that makes you feel different from everyone else.

_____

_____

_____

_____

Continued ➡

GrOUPS I BELONG TO (continued)

5. Think about one of the groups you belong to. Write down three things that make you proud to be a member of that group and three things that can make it difficult to belong to that group.

Group _____

What makes me proud to be in this group:

1. _____

_____

2. _____

_____

3. _____

_____

What makes it difficult for me to be in this group:

1. _____

_____

2. _____

_____

3. _____

_____

From *A Leader's Guide to The Courage to Be Yourself* by Al Desetta, M.A., and Sherrie Gammage, M.Ed., with Educators for Social Responsibility, copyright © 2006.
Free Spirit Publishing Inc., Minneapolis, MN; 866/703-7322; www.freespirit.com. This page may be photocopied for individual, classroom, or small group work only.

Being Different

A Stranger in a Strange School, by Esther Rajavelu

Pages 13–17 in *The Courage to Be Yourself*

overview

Story Summary

On arriving from India, Esther experiences a very uncomfortable first day of school in the United States—everyone else seems normal and she feels weird. But over time she realizes that the labels "normal" and "weird" don't mean very much.

Prep Work

- Put the session's agenda on the board or flip chart (see Preview).
- On the board or flip chart, write the discussion questions from the activity (see Activity).

Objectives

Group members will:

- identify standards in the story that young people used to judge Esther as "different"
- identify how those standards apply in their school

Themes

- Listening skills, active listening
- Point of view
- Caring communication
- Stereotyping

Links to the Academic Curriculum

- Literacy
- Public speaking and listening

THE SESSION

Preview

Preview the agenda by telling the group that today you will discuss the issue of being different and how it leads to labeling. To do this, you will engage in the activities on this agenda:

Agenda: Being Different

Reading: "A Stranger in a Strange School"
Gathering: Finding Partners
Activity: Are Labels Fair?
- Summary
- Pair share
- Large group discussion
Closing: Checking Out What We've Learned

Gathering: Finding Partners

This activity not only serves as a gathering, but also puts group members in pairs for the activity that follows. It helps the group begin to form a community, because most group members will work with partners different from the ones they usually hang out or work with.

1. **Introduction.** Tell the group that today you will review the story everyone read for the session ("A Stranger in a Strange School") and discuss why kids separate themselves from other kids. When young people do this, it can set the stage for bullying and harassment. Tell group members they will react to the story by sharing their responses with another person in a pair share.

2. **Choose partners.** Tell the group members to find a partner whose birthday is in the month that either precedes or follows theirs. This will force most group members to choose a partner who they don't usually hang out with. Give group members two minutes to find a partner.

Activity: Are Labels Fair?

1. **Summary.** Ask a volunteer to summarize "A Stranger in a Strange School" in two to three sentences. You may wish to write the story summary on the board or chart paper as a reminder for the group. You may copy the summary provided on page 23 or a summary the group comes up with.

2. **Pair share.** Break the group into pairs for a pair share. (See page 135 for a complete description of pair shares.) Read aloud the first of the following discussion questions. Allow one minute for one partner in each pair to answer the question, while the other partner listens. When the minute is up, have the second partner respond for one minute while the first listens. After the second minute is up, read the second question and allow another two minutes—one for each partner—for responses.
   Questions:

- *Have you ever felt, like Esther, that everyone else was "normal" and you were the "weird" one? What made you feel that way? Did anyone reach out to make you feel more comfortable?*

- *In your school or neighborhood, how are "normal" and "weird" defined? Are these labels fair? How do you define "normal" and "weird"?*

3. **Large group discussion.** Ask for volunteers to share their answers to each individual question with the whole group by asking the questions in the order they were introduced and eliciting two or three responses per question. Pay attention to the ways answers are similar to and different from

one another. Use responses as a jumping-off point for a larger discussion of labels, especially the labels of "normal" and "weird." If you feel comfortable doing so, you may relate a personal anecdote about your experience with these labels. (Sharing your own stories can be helpful in creating a dynamic discussion.)

Closing: Checking Out What We've Learned

Ask for volunteers to share an opinion, idea, or point of view they've changed or will reconsider as a result of today's discussion.

Assign a story from *The Courage to Be Yourself* to be read for your group's next meeting.

What Is Harassment?

Afraid to Learn, by Omar Morales

Pages 19–22 in *The Courage to Be Yourself*

overview

Story Summary

Omar is teased and bullied in school, and at one point gets beat up by another student. As a result, he finds it hard to concentrate in class. Although he is uncomfortable going to school, Omar doesn't engage in negative behavior or drop out.

Materials

- Flip chart paper
- Markers
- Handout: Types of Harassment

Prep Work

- Make a copy of the Types of Harassment handout (page 30) for everyone in your group.
- Put the session's agenda on the board or flip chart (see Preview).

Objectives

Group members will:

- define harassment
- identify different types of harassment
- discuss the effects of harassment on targets and on the school community

Themes

- Analysis of conflict
- Active listening
- Appreciation for differences
- Point of view and perspective taking
- Emotional literacy: positive expression of feelings

Links to the Academic Curriculum

- Public speaking and listening
- Cooperative learning

THE SESSION

Preview

Preview the agenda by telling the group that today you will discuss the issue of harassment. To do this you will engage in the activities on this agenda:

Agenda: What Is Harassment?

Reading: "Afraid to Learn"
Gathering: Defining Harassment
Activity: Examples of Harassment
- Summary
- Large group discussion: harassment in the story
- Large group discussion: harassment at your school
- Review
- Handout
Closing: Checking Out What We've Learned

Gathering: Defining Harassment

1. **Introduction.** Introduce the session by saying: *To begin our discussion of harassment, we'll talk about what it means to be harassed, so later we can begin to think about what we can do about it. To start this discussion, we will define harassment as a group by creating a web to organize our thinking.*

2. **Harassment web.** On the board or flip chart paper, draw a circle and write the word *harassment* in the center with lines extending out from the circle. Ask group members what thoughts, words, feelings, and behaviors come to mind when they hear the word. Write each idea on a different line. (See page 136 for a complete description of webbing.)

3. **Large group discussion.** Ask for volunteers to define harassment based on the ideas from the web. Write their definitions on the board. Then put the following definition on the board and compare it to the group's definition: *Harassment is any inappropriate, unwanted, or cruel behavior that makes someone feel uncomfortable, embarrassed, or threatened.*

Point out that harassment is sometimes a single act, but more often is composed of repeated acts performed over time. The target (the person being harassed) and the aggressor (the person doing the harassment) do not have to agree about what is happening. The aggressor might say, "I was just joking," but if the target feels threatened, then it's harassment.

Explain that harassment is related to issues of power. Aggressors can exert verbal, social, or physical power over a target.

Activity: Examples of Harassment

1. **Summary.** Ask for volunteers to summarize "Afraid to Learn" in two to three sentences. You may wish to write the story summary on the board or chart paper as a reminder for the group. You may copy the summary provided on page 26 or a summary the group comes up with.

2. **Large group discussion: harassment in the story.** Write three list headings on the board or flip chart: "Verbal harassment," "Social harassment," and "Physical harassment." Ask the group to name examples of harassment Omar

faced himself or saw happening in his school. Ask them to say whether each example was verbal, social, or physical harassment. As they name the examples, add them to the appropriate list. Examples from the story include:

Verbal harassment
  name-calling
  put-downs
  threats
Social harassment
  exclusion
  humiliation
Physical harassment
  intimidation
  unwanted touching
  robbery
  assault

3. **Large group discussion: harassment at your school.** Ask group members to expand the three lists by volunteering kinds of harassment they have experienced or witnessed at school. List what they volunteer under the categories you already have compiled from Omar's story. The lists might expand to include the following:

Verbal harassment
  sexual harassment (verbal)
  comments on people's appearance
Social harassment
  rumors and gossip
  ignoring people
  mean tricks
  racism
  sexism
Physical harassment
  threatening gestures
  sexual harassment (physical)
  destroying property
  pushing
  display of weapons

4. **Review.** Reviewing the lists, ask group members to identify the four or five most common forms of harassment they experience or witness at school. Place an asterisk next to these on the lists.

5. **Handout.** Distribute the Types of Harassment handout and read through it together. Ask if anyone has any questions or would like to discuss any of the definitions.

Closing: Checking Out What We've Learned

Read the following sentence aloud, filling in the blank with your answer. In a go-round, ask each group member to do the same.

As we worked together, I kept thinking about _____.

Assign a story from *The Courage to Be Yourself* to be read for your group's next meeting.

Session extensions

The following activities can be incorporated into the previous session, if time permits, or can be conducted at the following meeting as a separate session.

Activity: Effects of Harassment

1. **Review.** Briefly review "Afraid to Learn" and the definition of harassment from the previous session.

2. **Concentric circles.** Divide teens into two equal groups by having them count off. (If you don't have two equal groups, you can pair with one group member.) Group members should form pairs, either facing each other in two parallel rows or by forming a larger circle of group members around a smaller, inside circle. (See page

133 for a complete description of concentric circles.) Read the following question out loud and give pairs one minute to discuss it:

- *Why do you think Omar was the target of harassment?*

Ask for volunteers to share their ideas. After a brief large group discussion, the outside circle should move one to three places to the left, so that group members are paired with a new partner. Read the next question. Again, give the pairs one minute to discuss and then share their answers with the whole group.

- *How was Omar affected by the harassment?*

Repeat this process for the following questions, having the group rotate in order to switch partners for each.

- *Why does Omar think some kids bully others? Do you agree or disagree with him? Why?*
- *What strengths did Omar show in dealing with his situation?*

Activity: Harassment and the School Community

After the group has been reseated, brainstorm responses to the following questions. Record the group's ideas on the board or flip chart.

- *How did the harassment affect Omar? What are some other ways harassment could affect a target?*
- *Did Omar feel protected or safe at school? Why or why not?*
- *How does harassment affect our/your school community?*
- *What could be done—either by students or adults—to decrease teasing and bullying and make kids feel safer at school?*
- *If kids tease other kids to get respect, are there things kids or adults could do to give them respect in better ways?*

TYPES OF HARASSMENT

Sexual harassment is unwanted sexual comments or actions. That includes unwanted touching, gestures, insults that have to do with sex, and persistent compliments that have to do with physical appearance. It also includes spreading sexually oriented rumors. Comments or actions directed toward a person or group that make witnesses uncomfortable can also be sexual harassment. Sexually harassing comments can be spoken or written. They can be made using graffiti, pagers, cell phones, instant messages, blogs, Web sites, or email—or through other forms of communication.

Racial harassment includes racist comments and attacks on someone's skin color, ethnicity, native language, or national origin.

Gender-related harassment, also called homophobic harassment, includes attacks on people who are or are perceived to be lesbian, gay, bisexual, or transgendered (LGBT) because of their real or perceived gender orientation. Examples include calling someone a *fag*, a *dyke*, or using *gay* or *queer* as an insult.

Religious harassment includes attacks on someone's religious beliefs, practices, or affiliation.

Size-based harassment means taunting someone because of his or her height or weight.

Ability-level harassment includes insulting a person because of a real or assumed physical or mental ability or disability. Examples include calling someone *retard*, *dummy, nerd,* or *geek* or making fun of individuals who use a wheelchair, a hearing aid, or glasses, or are academically above or below average.

Harassment based on class includes teasing or ridiculing someone based on the amount of money or possessions that person has or doesn't have.

Harassment based on looks may include calling someone *ugly* or referring to someone as a *dog*.

From *A Leader's Guide to The Courage to Be Yourself* by Al Desetta, M.A., and Sherrie Gammage, M.Ed., with Educators for Social Responsibility, copyright © 2006. Free Spirit Publishing Inc., Minneapolis, MN; 866/703-7322; www.freespirit.com. This page may be photocopied for individual, classroom, or small group work only.

How Do We Experience Conflict?

Sticking with Your "Own Kind," by Cassandra Thadal

Pages 23–27 in *The Courage to Be Yourself*

overview

Story Summary

Cassandra faces pressure from her friends to stop hanging out with kids from other races and ethnic groups. But Cassandra finds a way to keep her friends and still be close to people who are "different."

Prep Work

- Put the session's agenda on the board or flip chart (see Preview).

Objectives

Group members will:

- identify the messages they have received about conflict
- listen to others share their experiences with conflict
- make connections between their personal conflicts and conflicts they observe in the larger society

Themes

- Caring and effective communication
- Point of view and perspective taking
- The roles of empathy and positive expression of feelings

Links to the Academic Curriculum

- Public speaking and listening

THE SESSION

Preview

Preview the agenda by telling the group that today you will discuss the group's experiences with and attitudes toward conflict. To do this you will engage in the activities on this agenda:

Agenda: How Do We Experience Conflict?

Reading: "Sticking with Your 'Own Kind'"
Gathering: Conflict in Our Lives
Activity: Common Messages and Attitudes
　About Conflict
　• Summary
　• Discussion points
　• Microlab
　• Large group discussion
Closing: Checking Out What We've Learned

Gathering: Conflict in Our Lives

1. **Introduction.** The goal of this session is to help group members examine, understand, and question their attitudes toward conflict. Introduce the session by telling the group that today you will discuss conflict in your lives and how your past experiences affect your responses to bullying, teasing, harassment, or being excluded by others.

2. **Pair share.** Break the group into pairs for a pair share. (See page 135 for a complete description of pair shares.) Read the following statement and allow one minute for one person in each pair to talk, without interruption: *When I get into a conflict, I usually _____.*

　After one minute, call time and allow the second partner in each pair to respond for one minute.

Activity: Common Messages and Attitudes About Conflict

1. **Summary.** Ask for volunteers to summarize "Sticking with Your 'Own Kind,'" the assigned reading for this session, in two to three sentences. You may wish to write the story summary on the board or chart paper as a reminder for the group. You may copy the summary provided on page 31 or a summary the group comes up with.

2. **Discussion points.** Tell the group: *Conflict can be a physical fight, but it can also be non-physical. Non-physical conflict can be a disagreement among individuals or groups. Sometimes non-physical conflict is internal, like when you struggle with a difficult decision.*

　All people experience conflict, but people's attitudes and beliefs about conflict vary. Some are taught to believe all conflict is bad and it should be avoided at all costs. Others are encouraged to deal with conflict openly and fairly. And still others believe the only way to deal with conflict is to use power over someone else in order to get their way. These people may think power not only helps them get what they want but also earns respect.

3. **Microlab.** Divide teens into groups of three for a microlab (if the number of group members is not divisible by three, make groups of four with the extra group members). This is a timed speaking and listening activity in which group members practice good listening skills. (See page 134 for a complete description of microlabs.)

　Explain that each person will have one minute to talk to the other people in the group, answering a question you will read out loud. When that person is speaking, the others are only to listen, giving the speaker their full attention, no matter how tempted they are to respond.

Ask the first question listed below. Keep time for the group and let them know when one minute has passed. At that time, the next person in the group should answer the same question. When everyone in the group has had a turn, go through the same process with each subsequent question.

The focus during the microlab is on Cassandra—how she was perceived by her friends when she sat with kids from other races and ethnic groups, and her response to the conflict created by peer pressure. Note that the questions follow a progression: from messages about conflict, to how people handle conflict, to the larger issue of conflict at school.

Questions:

- *What message does Cassandra get from her friends about hanging out with kids from other races and ethnic groups?*

- *What message does Cassandra get from her friends about how to deal with this conflict?*

- *How is the way Cassandra handles this conflict similar to the way you handle conflict? How is it different?*

- *What types of conflicts do you face or see others facing at school?*

- *Do kids of different races, ethnic groups, or backgrounds mix together or stay separated? Why?*

- *Is it a problem if kids separate themselves? Why or why not?*

As you ask each question, it can be helpful to take a minute to give your own brief answer. This gives the group members a model of how to participate and stimulates their thinking.

4. **Large group discussion.** After the microlab is finished, ask for volunteers to share their answers with the whole group by asking the questions in the order they were introduced and eliciting two or three responses per question.

Closing: Checking Out What We've Learned

Conduct a brief large group discussion about the activity, being sure to cover two main points:

- The messages we receive from others—including family, friends, and the media—about conflict often have a big effect on how we deal with conflict. If we are aware of those messages, our options for responding to conflict won't be limited by them.

- Cassandra made positive choices. Discuss these and the positive choices people in the group have made in dealing with conflict.

Close this discussion by making a two-column chart. On one side have group members generate a list of conflicts in their school, and on the other side list how the conflicts might be addressed.

Assign a story from *The Courage to Be Yourself* to be read for your group's next meeting.

SESSION EXTENSION

This activity can be incorporated into the previous session, if time permits, or can be conducted at the following meeting as a separate session.

Activity: Group Stereotyping

1. **Review.** If you are conducting this extension at a later meeting, briefly review "Sticking with Your 'Own Kind'" with the group.

2. **Large group discussion.** Ask each person in your group to name a group they belong to or identify with, and write those groups on the board. If there is one group that many of them belong to, such as African American or female, encourage them to name other groups they belong to that they may share with fewer people in the group—for example, Muslim, soccer player, band member, style of dress, or choice in music—so you end up with a wider selection of groups. When you have a handful of groups listed, ask for volunteers to name stereotypes they have or have heard about the groups. Ask them where they think these stereotypes come from, how they affect people in those groups, and what can be done about changing stereotypes.

3. **Journals.** As a journal-writing assignment, ask your group members to describe how they've been affected by a stereotype of a group they identify with. What suggestions do they have for educating people about stereotypes? Give them three minutes to write. Remind them that they should not stop writing. (See page 134 for a complete description of journaling.) When time is up, ask for volunteers to share what they've written or to talk in a more general way about the topic.

We All Belong to Groups (Part 2)

Which Crowd Did You Pick? by Satra Wasserman

Pages 29–30 in *The Courage to Be Yourself*

overview

Story Summary

Satra is friends with kids in his school who play basketball, but when he decides to play handball and hang out with a new crowd, his old friends reject him.

Materials

- Flip chart paper
- Markers

Prep Work

- Put the session's agenda on the board or flip chart (see Preview).

Objectives

Group members will:

- discuss how groups or cliques affect attitudes and behavior

- relate the discussion of cliques to peer pressure
- identify the groups and cliques at their school

Themes

- Appreciation of differences and diversity
- Point of view and perspective taking
- Acknowledging the importance and impact of groups

Links to the Academic Curriculum

- Cooperative learning
- Public speaking and listening

THE SESSION

Preview

Preview the agenda by telling the group that today you will discuss the issue of how and why young people belong to groups, and what impact group membership has on them. To do this you will engage in the activities on this agenda:

Agenda: We All Belong to Groups

Reading: "Which Crowd Did You Pick?"
Gathering: Reading the Story
Activity: Mapping the Groups in School
- Summary
- Small group discussion
- School map
- Large group discussion
Closing: Checking Out What We've Learned

Gathering: Reading the Story

Ask volunteers to read aloud "Which Crowd Did You Pick?" which is short enough that this should take only a few minutes. You may have a few volunteers read a couple paragraphs each.

Activity: Mapping the Groups in School

1. **Summary.** Ask for volunteers to summarize "Which Crowd Did You Pick?" in two to three sentences. You may wish to write the story summary on the board or chart paper as a reminder for the group. You may copy the summary provided on page 35 or a summary the group comes up with. (Note: Even though you have just read the story out loud, it's still a valuable exercise to have students summarize the story. Summarizing helps them to distill the main points of the story and focus on its themes.)

2. **Small group discussion.** Divide teens into groups of three to five. Put the first of the following questions on the board or flip chart and give the groups two or three minutes to discuss it. Then put the next question up, again allowing two or three minutes for small group discussion. Finally, put the third question up for discussion.

   - *Why did Satra's basketball friends exile him?*

   - *Have you ever been in a similar situation? If so, describe it.*

   - *What are the cliques in your school? Can you describe what they wear, the music they listen to, or other things about them?*

3. **School map.** Hand out chart paper and markers or crayons to each group. Have the groups draw a map of the school that indicates where various cliques hang out in or around the school. The maps can show the interior of the school, such as the lunchroom, in addition to areas outside the school where kids congregate by groups. On the map, group members should describe the cliques, including their dress, behavior, or other distinguishing features. (If you prefer, or if it's more appropriate, group members can map their neighborhoods.)

   Allow 10 to 12 minutes for the mapping activity. When time is up, post the maps on the board or around the room, or allow group members to circulate in the room to compare all the different versions of the maps.

4. **Large group discussion.** Conduct a group discussion around the following questions:

- *In what ways are the maps and descriptions of groups similar to and different from each other?*

- *Can a person belong to more than one group? Do you?*

- *How do other groups stereotype your group?*

- *Do people in different groups mingle? If not, why not?*

- *In what ways do labels and cliques limit or harm people? Can or should anything be done to prevent people from breaking apart into cliques, or isolating those who are different?*

Closing: Checking Out What We've Learned

Ask group members: *How did this session change your view of groups, either one you belong to or groups in general?* Put the following sentences on the board and ask for volunteers to complete them: *Before this discussion, I didn't know _____. After this discussion, I know _____.*

Assign a story from *The Courage to Be Yourself* to be read for your group's next meeting.

Acceptance in Your Life
Fashion Un-Conscious, by Nadishia Forbes

Pages 31–35 in *The Courage to Be Yourself*

overview

Story Summary

Nadishia is originally from Jamaica and doesn't wear the latest fashions to school. She gets teased by two girls and eventually gets in a fight with them. Nadishia decides to dress the way she likes and learns to look beyond appearances in getting to know people.

Materials

- Journals
- One basket or tray for each five or six people
- Poker chips (or other manipulative to represent "social currency"). You should have about 75 chips for each group of five or six.
- Handout: Acceptance Cards

Prep Work

- Photocopy the handout on pages 42–43 and cut out the Acceptance Cards. You'll need one set of cards for every five teens in your group.
- Put the session's agenda on the board or flip chart (see Preview).

Objectives

Group members will:

- reflect on how feeling accepted is often related to the possession or acquisition of material goods
- reflect on the ways that standards for acceptance can shift from one group or environment to another

Themes

- Undoing stereotypes and bias
- Point of view and perspective taking
- Preventing or stopping harassment

Links to the Academic Curriculum

- Math: probability and projections
- Speaking
- Listening

THE SESSION

Preview

Preview the agenda by telling the group that today you will discuss the ways that a person's family circumstances or financial status can contribute to harassment as well as to acceptance, and confront stereotypes associated with those circumstances. To explore these topics you will engage in the activities on this agenda:

Agenda: Acceptance in Your Life

Reading: "Fashion Un-Conscious"
Gathering: Journals
Activity: Finding Acceptance
  • Summary
  • Large group discussion
  • Acceptance cards
  • Large group discussion
Closing: Checking Out What We've Learned

Gathering: Journals

Ask group members to respond in their journals to each of the following four sets of questions. (See page 134 for a complete description of journaling.) Read each set of questions and allow one to two minutes for group members to respond before reading the next.
  Questions:

• *Does being accepted by others help you feel good about yourself? Why or why not?*

• *How do things like having the "right clothes" or looking or acting like everyone else help people fit in?*

• *Write about a time when you felt like you fit in. What made you fit in?*

• *Write about a time when you did not fit in and felt like an outsider. Why did you feel that way? How did it affect your self-esteem? How did it turn out?*

Activity: Finding Acceptance

1. **Summary.** Ask volunteers to summarize "Fashion Un-Conscious" in two to three sentences. You may wish to write the story summary on the board or chart paper as a reminder for the group. You may copy the summary provided on page 38 or a summary the group comes up with.

2. **Large group discussion.** Tell the group: *Nadishia is an immigrant from Jamaica. Because she is relatively poor compared to the other kids in her school, she cannot afford the same name-brand clothes as her new peers and is not accepted by them. Quite often, young people don't have control over what material goods they have, such as the clothes they wear. They also can't control other circumstances, such as their race or athletic ability. Despite that, young people can gain or lose acceptance among their peers based on these things. Sometimes people also discriminate and harass others based on material and outward circumstances.*

  Conduct a group discussion around the following discussion questions:

• *What are some standards that acceptance is based on at your school or in your community? In other words, why are some kids accepted and others not?*

• *Can you think of another school, community, or peer group in which the standards for acceptance might be different? For example, maybe a certain brand of shoes gets you credibility with one group but gets you laughed at by another.*

3. **Acceptance cards.** Divide teens into groups of five or six. Have each group arrange their chairs in a circle and ask for a volunteer from each group to be the game director. Distribute at least 75 poker chips to each game director. Distribute a basket filled with Acceptance Cards to each group. The cards should be face down in the basket. Each group should get an identical set of Acceptance Cards.

Have the members of each group take turns selecting a card from the basket and reading it to their group. Each card describes a life situation. As each card is selected, the group discusses it and decides how many chips it is worth. Chips represent a sort of social currency—the more chips a person has, the more accepted that person is by peers. Each card can be worth anywhere from zero to 10 chips. A card worth zero chips would make a teen a complete social outcast, and a card worth 10 would make a teen extremely popular. After the card's chip value is agreed upon by the group, the game director writes the chip value on the card and gives the group member who selected the card the appropriate number of chips.

The basket is then passed to the next person in the group, who also selects a card and reads it aloud to the group. After a discussion of that card's value, the game director awards chips to the group member and records the value on the card. Have group members continue this process until the cards are gone. Allow 20 minutes for the groups to read cards and discuss their values.

4. **Large group discussion.** After the card activity is finished, conduct a discussion with the whole group about their experience. Start by asking for volunteers to discuss how many chips they ended up

with and why. Then go through each Acceptance Card and ask how much value each group awarded to each card. Pay particular attention to cards that received very different values from different groups. For example, one group might give a lot of chips to the person who works an after-school job, because it teaches responsibility and helps him earn money, while another group might award that same card fewer chips because a job takes time away from doing homework or from socializing. What does this say about our standards for acceptance?

If these points don't come up in the discussion, bring them up:

- *The more wealth people have in a society, the more things they can purchase to enhance their status and gain more acceptance.*

- *Nadishia was, to an extent, at the mercy of circumstances beyond her control—the culture she came from, the school she attended, and the students who happened to be in her class.*

- *Things like native language, ethnicity, gender, and race are beyond an individual's control. We are all born with a certain set of "chips."*

- *Sometimes, people try to buy acceptance. But purchasing acceptance can only go so far. Nadishia didn't feel more accepted when she wore brand-name sneakers.*

Ask the group:

- *How much control did you have over the cards you were dealt?*

- *How much control do you feel you have over whether you're accepted by others?*

- *Regardless of your social or material circumstances, what are some healthy ways to acquire acceptance?*

Closing: Checking Out What We've Learned

Popcorn-style sharing. Form a large circle with the group and explain how popcorn-style sharing works: everyone may share their thoughts at any time, and there is no pressure to participate. (See page 135 for a complete description of popcorn-style sharing.) Ask volunteers to respond to the following question:

What is the relationship between being accepted and self-esteem?

Assign a story from *The Courage to Be Yourself* to be read for your group's next meeting.

ACCEPTANCE CARDS

One of your parents/ guardians lost his or her job and you can't afford to buy new clothes. _____ chips	One of your parents/ guardians has a high-paying job and the other stays at home. _____ chips	You live with one parent/ guardian, who is on public assistance. _____ chips
You wear thrift store clothes. _____chips	You're very good at sports and will be going to college on an athletic scholarship. _____ chips	You get a big allowance each week. _____ chips

ACCEPTANCE CARDS (continued)

You have an after-school job. _____ chips	You're in foster care. _____ chips	You're in the racial majority at your school. _____ chips
English is your second language and you speak it with a heavy accent. _____ chips	You live in a high-crime neighborhood. _____ chips	Your parents/guardians bought you a new car to drive to school. _____ chips
You bought your own used car with money you earned. _____ chips	You live in a gated community. _____ chips	School is easy for you and you get good grades without really trying. _____ chips

Interrupting Bullying and Harassment

Lighten Up on Heavy People, by Jennifer Cuttino

Pages 37–38 in *The Courage to Be Yourself*

overview

Story Summary

Since junior high, Jennifer has been teased for being overweight. Fortunately, she has friends who accept her and come to her defense.

Materials

- Flip chart paper and markers
- Signs labeled Target, Aggressor, Instigator, Bystander, and Ally
- Definitions of the roles written on the board or flip chart paper (see page 45)
- Ball of yarn
- Timer or watch
- Handout: Being a Good Ally

Prep Work

- Before this session, use chart paper to post signs labeled Target, Aggressor, Instigator, Bystander, and Ally in different areas of the room.

- Make a copy of the handout Being a Good Ally (page 47–48) for everyone in your group.

- Put the session's agenda on the board or flip chart (see Preview).

Objectives

Group members will:

- identify and define roles that individuals play in situations involving harassment
- discuss nonviolent allying behaviors

Themes

- Anti-harassment and bullying
- Perspective taking
- Social responsibility

Links to the Academic Curriculum

- Listening
- Public speaking
- Drama

THE SESSION

Preview

Preview the agenda by telling the group that today you will discuss how to stop bullying and harassment. To do this, you will engage in the activities on this agenda:

Agenda: Interrupting Bullying and Harassment

Reading: "Lighten Up on Heavy People"
Gathering: Defining Harassment
Activity 1: Roles in a Harassment Situation
• Summary
• Large group discussion
Activity 2: Questioning Roles
• Groups
• Rotation stations
• Large group discussion
Closing: Checking Out What We've Learned

Gathering: Defining Harassment

Use popcorn-style sharing to help the group come up with a definition of harassment. Form a large circle with the group and explain how popcorn-style sharing works: everyone may share their thoughts at any time, and there is no pressure to participate. (See page 135 for a complete description of popcorn-style sharing.) Use the questions below as prompts:

• **What is the definition of harassment?** (After the group has shared their responses, you may wish to read the definition on page 27. Ask group members to comment on how this definition is different from theirs, if at all.)

• **What are some examples of harassing behavior?**

• **What are some different types of harassment?**

Activity 1: Roles in a Harassment Situation

1. **Summary.** Ask for volunteers to summarize "Lighten Up on Heavy People" in two to three sentences. You may wish to write the story summary on the board or chart paper as a reminder for the group. You may copy the summary provided on page 44 or a summary the group comes up with.

2. **Large group discussion.** Ask the group to describe the different roles people can play in a harassment situation. List their responses on the board or chart paper, and then compare them with the ones below:

Target: A person or group being harassed.

Aggressor: A person who taunts, threatens, humiliates, victimizes, or physically harms the target. Also known as a bully.

Instigator: A person who spreads rumors, gossip, or makes up things to encourage others to harass the target. Instigating can be done verbally, on the Internet, through instant messages or text messages, or through graffiti in public places.

Bystander: A person who either witnesses or knows that the target is being harassed, and does or says nothing. Bystanders may be adults or even a friend of the target.

Ally: A person who stands up for the target by defending her or him nonviolently and by challenging the aggressor's attacks.

Discuss what it means to be an ally. Emphasize that an ally is peaceful and nonviolent. Point out examples of peaceful and nonviolent struggles, such as the Civil

Rights movement of the 1950s–1960s, when white, Latino, Native American, and other individuals allied with the African-American community as they sought civil rights. What were some of the methods these allies used to help correct a social injustice or wrong-doing? (Mention some examples such as nonviolent marches, boycotts, standing up for victims, and speaking out against Jim Crow laws.) Ask the group: *How do these examples apply to the issue of harassment in schools?*

Activity 2: Questioning Roles

1. **Groups.** Divide the teens into five groups and direct each group to stand at one of the signs you have posted in the room. Give each group a sheet of flip chart paper that has one of the following questions written on it. Each group should have the question that is appropriate for its role.

   - What can **targets** do when they are being harassed? Where can they get help?
   - What kinds of consequences should there be for **aggressors** in school?
   - Why do people become **instigators**? What can you do to prevent people from instigating conflict and social drama?
   - How can **bystanders** become allies?
   - How can **allies** confront instigators and work to educate the school about harassment?

2. **Rotation stations.** Give the groups two minutes to brainstorm responses to the questions and to record them on the flip chart paper. At the end of two minutes, have all the groups stand up and rotate to another station (or role), leaving their chart paper behind. At their new stations, the groups should take another two minutes to read the new question and to add their ideas to the list started by the first group. Then have them rotate again. Continue this process until each group has had the opportunity to brainstorm on all of the questions and has returned to the station where they began.

3. **Large group discussion.** Ask volunteers from each group to read the questions and responses out loud to the large group. Discuss the fact that most people play more than one of these roles every day. For example, a person may act as an ally in one circumstance but as an instigator when in a different crowd.

Closing: Checking Out What We've Learned

1. **Handout.** Distribute the handout Being a Good Ally. Give the group a few moments to silently review it.

2. **Support web.** Form a large circle. To start the activity, hold the ball of yarn and say: *To be a better ally, I will _____ ,* and finish the sentence. Then, holding the end piece of yarn, hand or toss the ball of yarn to a group member and ask that person say, "To be a better ally, I will _____," and finish the sentence. That person then tosses the ball to someone across the circle, while holding onto his or her part of the yarn. The next person should also complete the sentence and pass the ball of yarn. Continue this process until everyone is holding a strand of yarn.

   Assign a story from *The Courage to Be Yourself* to be read for your group's next meeting.

BEING A GOOD ALLY

Without allies, the cycle of harassment continues unchecked. Here are a few things to consider when you confront or witness teasing, harassment, and bullying.

- Ignoring isolated incidents may work, but a consistent problem of harassment will probably continue unless you act to stop it.

- Many targets of harassment laugh in the beginning because they are nervous or embarrassed. They may believe or hope they can just "laugh it off." Often aggressors and bystanders misinterpret the laughter, thinking it means the target doesn't mind.

- When you feel uncomfortable or threatened, speak up in a strong, confident, and assertive voice. You have the right not to be harassed! Tell the aggressor firmly, "Don't talk to/touch me like that. I don't like it," "Don't go there. I'm not starting with you—so don't start with me," or "That's harassment. If you don't stop, I will report it."

- Often, the harasser is angry about something (though being angry does not justify harassment) that has nothing to do with the target. It may help to ask calmly, "What's up? What are you angry about?" or "Why are you doing that?" Using insults or threats escalates the problem rather than helps to solve it, and can get you in trouble instead of the person who started it.

- If you choose to confront someone who is bullying or harassing you, find allies who will speak up without using threats to support you. This does not mean finding someone bigger to intimidate the harasser, because this has the potential to escalate the problem. Act as an ally for allies.

- If you're nervous about nonviolently confronting a person who is an aggressor or an instigator, that's a good indication it's time to inform adults about the problem.

Continued ➞

Being an ally for others:

⫸ If you witness people being harassed, help them by being a good ally. Speak up without putting anyone down. Try saying something like, "Let's knock it off," "That's just mean, there's no reason to go there," "I think that went a bit too far," or "We don't say that kind of stuff here."

⫸ You can make similar comments to people who are instigating, saying, "I don't think that's funny," or "That's just a rumor. Drop it."

⫸ When speaking to the person being harassed, say, "I think they're being mean," or "I think they are looking for trouble. This isn't worth it. Let's get out of here."

⫸ It is especially effective if two or more allies speak up, because it helps prevent the harasser from turning on a single ally. If you see an ally who is getting picked on, act as an ally for that person and the target by saying something like, "This is getting real old. Can you just drop it already?"

If the harassment continues, make sure to tell a teacher, counselor, parent, or other trusted adult. You have the right to a safe environment, and teachers, counselors, and administrators are required by law to respond.

Types of Peer Pressure

Losing My Friends to Weed, by Jamel A. Salter

Pages 39–42 in *The Courage to Be Yourself*

overview

Story Summary

Jamel has close relationships with his child-hood friends, until they start smoking marijuana. He refuses to smoke with them and his friends abandon him. Jamel wishes the friendships could go back to the way they used to be.

Materials

- Flip chart paper, markers, and tape
- Chart paper with each peer pressure definition
- Four peer pressure signs, prepared before session meeting

Prep Work

- Make a sign, or write on the board or flip chart, a definition of peer pressure (see Activity 1, page 50).
- Make four signs labeled Positive Direct, Positive Indirect, Negative Direct, and Negative Indirect, with their definitions (see page 50).
- Put the session's agenda on the board or flip chart (see Preview).

Objectives

Group members will:

- distinguish between the positive and negative aspects of peer pressure
- identify four types of peer pressure: positive direct, positive indirect, negative direct, and negative indirect
- identify ways to deal with peer pressure
- practice refusal skills

Themes

- Point of view and perspective taking
- Conflict analysis
- Alternative responses to conflict

Links to the Academic Curriculum

- Drug abuse prevention training and workshops
- Safe and drug-free schools
- Drama and theater

THe SeSSION

Preview

Preview the agenda by telling the group that today you will discuss the various types of peer pressure. To do this, you will engage in the activities on this agenda:

Agenda: Types of Peer Pressure

Reading: "Losing My Friends to Weed"
Gathering: Friend Pressure
Activity 1: What Is Peer Pressure?
  • Summary
  • Large group discussion
Activity 2: Ways to Say No
  • Large group brainstorm
Activity 3: Practice in Dealing with Peer Pressure
  • Role-play
  • Large group discussion
Closing: Checking Out What We've Learned

Gathering: Friend Pressure

Ask group members to pair up with someone sitting near them. (See page 135 for a complete description of pair shares.) Read aloud the first of the following discussion questions. Allow one minute for one partner in each pair to answer the question, while the other partner listens without interruption. When the minute is up, have the second partner respond for one minute while the first listens. After the second minute is up, read the second question and allow another two minutes—one for each partner in each pair—for responses.

Questions:

• **Describe a time when a friend pressured you to do something positive (for example, study for a test or join a sports team).**

• **Talk about a time when a friend pressured you to do something negative (for example, smoke cigarettes or cheat on a test).**

Activity 1: What Is Peer Pressure?

1. **Summary.** Ask for volunteers to summarize "Losing My Friends to Weed" in two to three sentences. You may wish to write the story summary on the board or chart paper as a reminder for the group. You may copy the summary provided on page 49 or a summary the group comes up with.

2. **Large group discussion.** Post a definition of *peer pressure*, such as: **Peer pressure is when your friends or other people your age try to influence your behavior or actions.** Discuss with group members the fact that most people want to fit in and feel like they belong to a group. Because of that feeling, sometimes people do things they normally wouldn't do in order to fit in. Explain that peer pressure can be positive or negative depending on what your friends are pressuring you to do. Ask for volunteers to share some of the peer pressure situations they discussed in the pair share.

   Next, post the following definition of *direct peer pressure*: **You are specifically asked or pressured to do something that you may or may not want to do. Direct peer pressure can be positive or negative.** Ask group members to give examples of direct peer pressure from Jamel's story. (Jamel's friends pressure him to smoke with them. His friends then call him names when he doesn't smoke.) Ask the group whether these examples are positive or negative direct peer pressure.

The activities in Session 8 are adapted from *Peer 2 Peer: A Guide to Peer Education*, by Heather Coulehan (Anchorage, AK: Anchorage School District Safe & Drug Free Schools, 2002), and used with permission.

Now post the following definition of *indirect peer pressure:* **No one directly asks you to do something but you still feel pressured to go along with the group. Indirect peer pressure can be positive or negative.** Ask the group to give examples of indirect peer pressure from Jamel's story. (Jamel's friends put in money to buy marijuana, they smoke in front of him, and they exclude him from basketball games.) Ask the group whether these examples are positive or negative indirect peer pressure.

Activity 2: Ways to Say No

Large group brainstorm. Instruct the group to brainstorm other ways Jamel could have said no when his friends pressured him, directly and indirectly, to smoke marijuana. Record all ideas on flip chart paper for use in the next activity. Suggest these ideas if the group doesn't think of them:

- Say no with a friend
- Change the subject
- Remove yourself from the situation
- Shift responsibility (for example: "My coach says I can't" or "My mom needs me to watch my little brother")
- Be direct and firm
- Say no with humor or a joke
- Make an excuse or give a reason
- Suggest an alternative activity

Activity 3: Practice in Dealing with Peer Pressure

Although it can be easy to identify examples of peer pressure, it is often difficult to deal with peer pressure in real-life situations. The next activity will provide practice dealing with peer pressure situations.

1. **Role-play.** Divide teens into groups of three to five. Each group will design and demonstrate a role-play for the larger group that illustrates how Jamel was pressured and two ways he could have said no that are different from how he actually said no in the story. (See page 135 for a complete description of role-plays.)

   Provide the following guidelines:

   - Each group will have two minutes to present its role-play.
   - One person from each group will play Jamel, and the other group members will play his friends.
   - People playing Jamel's friends can role-play either direct or indirect peer pressure.

   Give groups five to seven minutes to come up with and practice their role-play. When they're ready, have the groups present their role-plays to the larger group.

2. **Large group discussion.** After each role-play, have the actors ask the audience the following questions:

   - *What type of peer pressure did you see?*
   - *Which ways to say no did we use? How effective were they?*
   - *Do you think this would work in real life? Why or why not?*

Closing: Checking Out What We've Learned

Read aloud the statement: ***It's not my fault. My friends made me do it.*** Ask the group to share their thoughts and feelings about this statement. What would be a more accurate statement to make based on the information from this session?

Assign a story from *The Courage to Be Yourself* to be read for your group's next meeting.

Responding to Conflict— What Do We Do? (Part 1)

Getting Guys off My Back, by Artiqua Steed

Pages 43–46 in *The Courage to Be Yourself*

overview

Story Summary

Artiqua is sexually harassed at school. One day, one of her tormentors crosses the line and she tries to fight him. He is punished by the school and doesn't bother Artiqua again, but she thinks schools need to do more to prevent this problem.

Materials

- Flip chart paper and markers
- Handouts: Conflict Cards, Six Conflict Resolution Styles, and Definition of Sexual Harassment

Prep Work

- Photocopy the Conflict Cards handout on page 55 and cut out the cards.
- Make a copy of the other two handouts, Six Conflict Resolution Styles (pages 56–57) and Definition of Sexual Harassment (page 58), for each person in your group.
- Put the session's agenda on the board or flip chart (see Preview).

Objectives

Group members will:

- identify their dominant and alternative conflict resolution styles
- discuss instances when it might be helpful to use different styles
- discuss the definition of sexual harassment

Themes

- Managing and resolving conflict
- Conflict analysis
- Caring and effective communication
- Point of view and perspective taking

Links to the Academic Curriculum

- Public speaking and listening

THE SESSION

Preview

Preview the agenda by telling the group that today you will discuss ways of responding to conflict. To do this, you will engage in the activities on this agenda:

Agenda: Responding to Conflict— What Do We Do?

Reading: "Getting Guys off My Back"
Gathering: Conflict Opinion Continuum
Activity 1: Conflict Resolution Styles
  • Summary
  • Large group discussion
Activity 2: Conflict Cards
  • Small group discussion
  • Large group discussion
Closing: Checking Out What We've Learned

Gathering: Conflict Opinion Continuum

Tell the group that you represent conflict. Have group members form a conflict opinion continuum by standing either close to or far from you to represent how comfortable they feel dealing with conflict. The closer a group member stands to you, the more comfortable he or she is confronting conflict. The farther away, the more he or she prefers to avoid conflict. (See page 134 for a complete description of opinion continuums.) When group members are in their places, ask for volunteers to describe why they chose to stand where they did.

Activity 1: Conflict Resolution Styles

1. **Summary.** Ask for volunteers to summarize "Getting Guys off My Back" in two to three sentences. You may wish to write the story summary on the board or chart paper as a reminder for the group. You may copy the summary provided on page 52 or a summary the group comes up with.

   Then ask the group: **What type of harassment was Artiqua experiencing? How do you know?**

2. **Large group discussion.** Distribute the Definition of Sexual Harassment handout. Ask group members to review or read aloud the handout and compare it to what happened to Artiqua in the story.

   Next, distribute the Six Conflict Resolution Styles handout and ask for a volunteer to read each style description aloud to the group. After each style is read, ask group members to suggest the strengths and weaknesses of that style. Emphasize the fact that because each conflict resolution style has it's strengths and weaknesses, the important thing is to recognize there are different methods of dealing with conflict and each person can choose the method that is right for each situation.

Activity 2: Conflict Cards

1. **Small group discussion.** Divide the group into threes and distribute one set of Conflict

Cards to each group. Each card describes a different conflict. Have group members take turns picking a card, reading it out loud, and telling their group which conflict resolution styles they think would be most and least effective in dealing with this situation, and why. Allow the groups 8–10 minutes to go through all the cards.

2. **Large group discussion.** Next, ask each group to prepare for a large group discussion by appointing a spokesperson and choosing one Conflict Card to discuss with the larger group. Give the groups three minutes to choose a card, the least and most effective style of dealing with that conflict, and their reasons why. Ask each group's spokesperson to present to the larger group her or his group's Conflict Card and the resolution styles they chose.

Close the activity by making the following discussion points:

- **Conflict is normal and natural.**
- **We all experience conflict.**
- **We all have choices about the way we choose to handle conflict.**

Closing: Checking Out What We've Learned

Popcorn-style sharing. Form a large circle with the group and explain how popcorn-style sharing works: everyone may share their thoughts at any time, and there is no pressure to participate. (See page 135 for a complete description of popcorn-style sharing.) Ask for volunteers to share answers to the following questions:

- **What style did Artiqua use to handle her conflict?**
- **What other styles could she have used to nonviolently and assertively deal with the harassment?**

Next, ask for volunteers to complete the following sentence stems, or make up their own analogies:

- Conflict is like a tornado because _____.
- Conflict is like a flower because _____.
- Conflict is like a river because _____.

If your group has trouble coming up with ideas, you can prompt them with the following examples: **Conflict is like a tornado because it can spin out of control. Conflict is like a flower because it unfolds. Conflict is like a river because it can run deep.**

Assign a story from *The Courage to Be Yourself* to be read for your group's next meeting.

CONFLICT CARDS

A male classmate repeatedly compliments Artiqua on her appearance, and it makes her uncomfortable.	You overhear a racial slur in the hallway and think the speaker is talking about the friend you are walking with.	As Artiqua is talking to friends, someone passes by and stops. She thinks Artiqua just insulted her.
Artiqua thinks her teacher has been unfair in grading an essay.	Artiqua's boss at the store where she works is always criticizing her. Her work never seems to be good enough.	Artiqua's mother is really mad. Artiqua was supposed to put the laundry in the washer this morning and she forgot.
Artiqua and two friends have spent 20 minutes arguing about what movie to see. Artiqua has had enough.	A friend wants to copy Artiqua's math homework. It took her an hour and a half to do it.	

SIX CONFLICT reSOLUTION STYLeS

1. Directing/Controlling
"My way or the highway."

When you use this style you cannot or will not bargain or give in. It can mean standing up for your rights and deeply held beliefs. It can also mean pursuing what you want at the expense of another person. You may be caught in a power struggle and can't see a way to negotiate for what you want.

Strengths of this style   1. _____

2. _____

Weaknesses of this style   1. _____

2. _____

2. Collaborating
"Let's sit down and work this out."

When you use this style you work with those you're in conflict with to satisfy the needs of everyone involved. You are interested in finding solutions and in maintaining—or even improving—the relationship. You see other people involved as partners rather than adversaries.

Strengths of this style   1. _____

2. _____

Weaknesses of this style   1. _____

2. _____

3. Compromising
"Let's both give a little" or "Something is better than nothing."

When you use this style you seek the middle ground. Both you and those you're in conflict with give up something for a solution that may satisfy each of you only partially.

Strengths of this style   1. _____

2. _____

Weaknesses of this style   1. _____

2. _____

Continued ➡

4. Accommodating

"Whatever you want is fine" or "It doesn't matter anyway."

When you use this style you yield to another's point of view, meeting the other person's needs while denying your own. You may give in to smooth the relationship, or to get your way another time.

Strengths of this style 1. _____

2. _____

Weaknesses of this style 1. _____

2. _____

5. Avoiding/Denying

"Let's skip it" or "Problem? I don't see a problem."

When you use this style you do not address the conflict and withdraw from the situation, or behave as though the situation were not happening. You leave it to others to deal with.

Strengths of this style 1. _____

2. _____

Weaknesses of this style 1. _____

2. _____

6. Appealing to a Greater Authority or a Third Party

"Help me out here."

When you use this style you turn to others whom you perceive as having more power, influence, authority, or wisdom to solve the conflict.

Strengths of this style 1. _____

2. _____

Weaknesses of this style 1. _____

2. _____

DEFINITION OF SEXUAL HARASSMENT

Sexual harassment is unwanted sexual comments or actions. That includes unwanted touching, gestures, insults that have to do with sex, and persistent compliments that have to do with physical appearance. It also includes spreading sexually oriented rumors. Comments or actions directed toward a person or group that make witnesses uncomfortable can also be sexual harassment. Sexually harassing comments can be spoken or written. They can be made using graffiti, pagers, cell phones, instant messages, blogs, Web sites, or email—or through other forms of communication.

Countering Stereotypes and Prejudice

My Boy Wanted a Boyfriend, by Odé A. Manderson

Pages 47–52 in *The Courage to Be Yourself*

Note: Talking with teens about sexual orientation and gender identity may trigger some group members to make inappropriate or offensive remarks. Before you proceed with the activity, you may want to review with the group your group's guidelines for respectful speaking and listening (see pages 12–13).

overview

Story Summary

Odé and Thomas meet at their summer job and become fast friends. Odé thinks Thomas might be gay, but doesn't want to make a big deal about it. When Thomas reveals he has a crush on Odé, Odé keeps his cool and doesn't reject Thomas as a friend.

Materials

- Flip chart paper and markers
- Journals
- Timer

Prep Work

- Put the session's agenda on the board or flip chart (see Preview).

Objectives

Group members will:

- reflect on their experiences with stereotyping others and feeling stereotyped or marginalized themselves
- examine the impact of stereotypes and prejudice
- discuss ways to look past stereotypes

Themes

- Appreciation of diversity
- Caring and effective communication
- Point of view and perspective taking

Links to the Academic Curriculum

- Character analysis
- Public speaking and listening

THE SESSION

Preview

Preview the agenda by telling the group that today you will discuss ways people can counter stereotypes and prejudice. To do this you will engage in the activities on this agenda:

Agenda: Countering Stereotypes and Prejudice

Reading: "My Boy Wanted a Boyfriend"
Gathering: What's Important in a Friend?
Activity 1: The Effects of Stereotyping
- Summary
- Brainstorm
- Journals
- Large group discussion
Activity 2: Odé's Response
- Large group discussion
- Microlab
Closing: Checking Out What We've Learned

Gathering: What's Important in a Friend?

Do a go-round, asking each group member to answer the question: **What is one important quality in a good friend?** (See page 133 for a complete description of go-rounds.)

Activity 1: The Effects of Stereotyping

1. **Summary.** Ask for volunteers to summarize "My Boy Wanted a Boyfriend" in two to three sentences. You may wish to write the story summary on the board or chart paper as a reminder for the group. You may copy the summary provided on page 59 or a summary the group comes up with.

2. **Brainstorm.** Ask your group to come up with a definition for *stereotype*, and write it on the board. (See page 133 for a complete description of brainstorming.) Then write the following definition on the board and compare it to the group's definition: ***Stereotype. An oversimplified generalization about a particular group, race, or gender; usually derogatory.***

3. **Journals.** Give your group three minutes to respond to the following prompt in their journals. (See page 134 for a complete description of journaling.)
   - ***Write about a time when you felt stereotyped. How did it feel? How did you react?***

4. **Large group discussion.** Conduct a large group discussion using the following questions as a guideline. Write responses on the board.
   - ***Does it matter if we stereotype people?***
   - ***What effects do stereotypes have on the person being stereotyped?***
   - ***What is the effect on the person doing the stereotyping?***
   - ***What is the impact of gay related or other types of stereotyping in your school climate? In your community?***

Activity 2: Odé's Response

1. **Large group discussion.** Read the following text aloud from "My Boy Wanted a Boyfriend." Have the group follow along on page 49 of *The Courage to Be Yourself*.

   "Thomas has something to say to you, but he's too shy to say it. Do you know what it is?"

I wasn't a total idiot. Or so I thought.

"Does it have anything to do with his sexual orientation?" I asked calmly.

"Yes, it does. That's not all, though. The reason why he had a hard time telling you was because he has a crush on you."

I was shocked. Butterflies suddenly fluttered in my gut, then turned into wild hornets, which felt like they were bursting through the wall of my stomach. Then a bright-colored spot appeared in front of my eyes. I was silent for a moment before I decided to say something. I was prepared to hear him tell me he was gay, not that he had it for me.

His cousin said that he liked me because of my looks and personality. I blinked hard.

"Tell him he has nothing to be shy about," I replied, trying to compose myself. "Put him on the phone."

I heard a faint "here" as she passed the receiver to Thomas.

"Yeah?"

"That's all you had to tell me? Look, you didn't have to tell me anything, so trusting me with that was strong of you. And this won't change our friendship, if that's what you're thinking. I'm cool."

Next, lead a discussion about Odé's response by using the following discussion questions: *Is it what you expected? Why? How did Odé go from angry to composed? What do you think Odé was thinking? How do you think Thomas felt after Odé said it wouldn't change their friendship?*

2. **Microlab.** Divide teens into groups of three for a microlab (if the number of group members in the group is not divisible by three, make groups of four with the extra group members). This is a timed speaking and listening activity in which group members practice good listening skills.

(See page 134 for a complete description of microlabs.)

Explain that each person will have one minute to talk to the other people in the group, answering a question you will read out loud. When one person is speaking, the others are only to listen, giving the speaker their full attention, no matter how tempted they are to respond.

Ask the first set of questions listed below. Keep time for the group and let group members know when one minute has passed. At that time, the next person in the group should answer the same questions. When everyone in the group has had a turn, go through the same process with the second set of questions.

Questions:

- *Thomas helped break Odé's stereotypes about gay people. Has anyone helped you break stereotypes you had about a group of people? How?*

- *Odé writes: "Why would someone go out of their way to hate on people because of how they live their lives? I think it's an exercise in stupidity. But I don't feel comfortable going up to strangers and calling them out." How do you react when you hear a stereotypical or hateful remark? How do you think you'll react in the future?*

Closing: Checking Out What We've Learned

In their journals, ask the group to write a list of five things they can do to combat stereotypes. If time permits, ask volunteers to share their lists.

Assign a story from *The Courage to Be Yourself* to be read for your group's next meeting.

session extension

The following activity can be incorporated into the previous session, if time permits, or can be conducted at the following meeting as a separate session.

Note: This extension invites group members to reflect on stereotypes about gay people. If you work with LGBT youth or with a gay-straight alliance (GSA) this activity may help generate an active, lively discussion. In a traditional classroom setting this activity may be difficult, as some LGBT or questioning group members could feel out-numbered and offended. Carefully consider the makeup of your group when deciding whether to do this extension.

Activity: Identifying Stereotypes

1. Brainstorming. Write: *Gay people are* _____ on the board. Encourage group members to voice not only their opinions, but generalizations and stereotypes from the media, other people they know, and anywhere else they've heard them. List all group member responses.

(See page 133 for a complete description of brainstorming.) Then invite volunteers to walk up to the board and circle the responses that are stereotypes.

2. Large group discussion. Lead a group discussion using the following prompts:

- *At the end of the story Odé writes: "Thomas made me realize that gay people aren't so stereotypical and have things in common with straight people. Thomas had some of the stereotypes in the way he walked and talked, but he was also quiet and thoughtful. He wasn't loud at all." What is your reaction to this? What is the difference between a stereotype and a character trait?*

- *How do organized groups (such as PFLAG*, GLSEN**, and school gay-straight alliances) combat stereotypes?*

- *What are some things you say (or wish you said) when you hear someone make a derogatory or offensive comment about LGBT people?*

*Parents, Families and Friends of Lesbians and Gays (www.pflag.org)
**Gay, Lesbian and Straight Education Network (www.glsen.org)

Resisting Conformity

Princess Oreo Speaks Out, by Dwan Carter

Pages 53–56 in *The Courage to Be Yourself*

overview

Story Summary

Because of her taste in music, use of large vocabulary words, and inability to dance, Dwan is teased by fellow blacks for "acting white." But Dwan is proud of who she is and won't change to please others.

Materials

- Flip chart paper and markers

Prep Work

- Put the session's agenda on the board or flip chart (see Preview).

Objectives

Group members will:

- discuss the pressure to conform to other people's expectations
- explore the consequences of being different
- reflect on how to be their own ally when expressing their individuality

Themes

- Exploring the internal nature of conflict
- Point of view and perspective taking
- Appreciation for differences

Links to the Academic Curriculum

- Public speaking and listening
- Point of view in literary work
- Character analysis

THE SESSION

Preview

Preview the agenda by telling the group that today you will discuss conforming to other people's expectations. To do this, you will engage in the activities on this agenda:

Agenda: Resisting Conformity

Reading: "Princess Oreo Speaks Out"
Gathering: What I Like About You
Activity 1: Expectations and Pressure
  • Summary
  • Pair share
  • Large group discussion
Activity 2: Reacting to Peer Pressure
  • Small group discussion
  • Large group discussion
Closing: Checking Out What We've Learned

Gathering: What I Like About You

This game is a variation of musical chairs. To start, have the group sit on the floor or on chairs in a tight-knit circle. Pick someone to stand in the middle of the circle to be the caller. The caller starts the game by saying, "What I like about you is that you [fill in the blank]." For example, "What I like about you is that you have brown eyes," "What I like about you is that you like Chinese food," or "What I like about you is that you play guitar." The caller must choose something that he or she also identifies with. For example, if the caller doesn't have brown eyes, then he or she cannot say, "What I like about you is that you have brown eyes."

After the caller says the sentence, everyone in the group who identifies with the statement (including the caller) stands up and moves through the middle of the circle to pick a spot

that someone else has left. (Those who don't identify with the statement remain seated in the circle.) Like musical chairs, the object of the game is to find a place to sit, but in this case, no one is eliminated from the game: whoever is left in the middle becomes the next caller. Now it's that person's turn to say, "What I like about you _____." Allow five to seven minutes for the game.

When finished, lead a brief discussion about how unique and complex each individual is. You may choose to use the following prompts:

• ***How did it feel to be the caller? Did you try to pick something you knew other people would identify with or did you try to come up with your most unique hobbies or qualities?***

• ***As the caller, you know if you pick something lots of people share your chances are better of finding a spot in the circle. Essentially, you know that fitting in with others feels "easier." How does this apply to your life?***

• ***While you were playing the game, were you ever surprised by who identified with the different statements?***

• ***Is there one trait or hobby that defines you?***

Activity 1: Expectations and Pressure

1. **Summary.** Ask volunteers to summarize "Princess Oreo Speaks Out" in two to three sentences. You may wish to write the story summary on the board or chart paper as a reminder for the group. You may copy the summary provided on page 63 or a summary the group comes up with.

2. **Pair share.** Divide the group into pairs and ask the first of the following questions. (See

page 135 for a complete description of pair shares.) Allow the pairs to have a dialogue on the question for two minutes, then ask for volunteers to share what they discussed with the larger group. After a few pairs have shared with the larger group, ask the next question and allow the pairs to have a dialogue about it. Again, ask for volunteers to share what they talked about when the time is up. Repeat the process for the third question.

Questions:

- *What are some of the assumptions that people made about Dwan?*

- *How was Dwan able to be herself despite what other people thought of her?*

- *What are the differences between stereoptyping, prejudice, and discrimination?*

3. **Large group discussion.** Write the following definitions on the board and compare them to group members' definitions.

- *Stereotype: An oversimplified generalization about a particular group, race, or gender—usually derogatory.*

- *Prejudice: A negative opinion or preconceived judgment based on ignorance or insufficient information; an irrational negative attitude against a person, group, race, or gender.*

- *Discrimination: Acting with bias toward an individual or group—often based on a stereotype.*

To help your teens make the connection between these terms and the pressure Dwan faces to conform, use the following discussion points:

- *When have you felt an internal conflict because of other people's expectations of how you should look or act? How did you handle it?*

- *Even if you have a strong sense of self, it can be hard not to let other people's expectations influence you. Name some of the people in your life who influence your views and actions. How do these people help guide you? How do they hold you back?*

Activity 2: Reacting to Peer Pressure

1. **Small group discussion.** Divide teens into groups of three or four. Have each group compile a list of ways they've encountered peer pressure to conform (for example, to listen to certain music or wear certain clothes). Then, ask group members to briefly describe a time they decided to conform and a time they resisted conforming.

2. **Large group discussion.** Ask the group:

- *How do you decide when to conform and when not to?*

- *Why do you think people tease their friends or pressure them to conform?*

- *What is so difficult about being different from your peers? What are the consequences? The benefits?*

Closing: Checking Out What We've Learned

In a go-round, have group members fill in the blanks in the following three statements. Remind them they have the right to pass.

"I am like others because _____."

"I am different from others because _____."

"I like myself because _____."

Assign a story from *The Courage to Be Yourself* to be read for your group's next meeting.

Session 12

Interrupting Prejudice and Stopping Verbal Abuse

I'm Both Arab and American, by Rana Sino

Pages 57–60 in *The Courage to Be Yourself*

overview

Story Summary

Rana, an Arab American, is offended when she hears her classmates insult all Arabs because of the September 11, 2001, terrorist attacks. She doesn't think people should blame an entire group of people for what a few did.

Materials

- Flip chart paper and markers
- Timer or watch
- Handout: Six Ways to Interrupt Prejudice and Verbal Abuse

Prep Work

- Make a copy of the Six Ways to Interrupt Prejudice and Verbal Abuse handout (pages 70–71) for everyone in your group.
- Put the session's agenda on the board or flip chart (see Preview).

Objectives

Group members will:

- think about times when they interrupted prejudice or witnessed someone else interrupting prejudice
- develop and review guidelines for interrupting prejudice and verbal abuse

Themes

- Managing and resolving conflict
- Appreciation of diversity
- Caring and effective communication

Links to the Academic Curriculum

- Character education: respect, personal integrity
- Perspective taking in a literary work
- Theater/drama/expressive arts

66

THE SESSION

Preview

Preview the agenda by telling the group that today you will discuss ways to interrupt prejudice and stop verbal abuse. To do this, you will engage in the activities on this agenda:

Agenda: Interrupting Prejudice and Stopping Verbal Abuse

Reading: "I'm Both Arab and American"
Gathering: Blaming Groups
Activity: Interrupting Prejudice and Verbal Abuse
- Summary
- Large group discussion
- Handout
- Large group discussion
Closing: Checking Out What We've Learned

Gathering: Blaming Groups

1. Pair share. Divide the group into pairs and read aloud the first of the following discussion questions. (See page 135 for a complete description of pair shares.) Allow one minute for one partner in each pair to answer the question, while the other partner listens. When the minute is up, have the second partner respond for one minute while the first listens. After the second minute is up, read the second question and allow another two minutes—one for each partner in each pair—for responses.

Questions:

- *Describe a time when you blamed a group of people or felt anger toward them because of what a few members of that group did.*

- *Describe a time when you were attacked or blamed because of the actions of a group you belonged to. (For example, as a teen,*

you may have heard people putting down all teenagers. Or you may have heard people putting down your racial or ethnic group.)

2. Large group discussion. Invite volunteers to share their responses with the group.

Activity 1: Interrupting Prejudice and Verbal Abuse

1. Summary. Ask volunteers to summarize "I'm Both Arab and American" in two to three sentences. You may wish to write the story summary on the board or chart paper as a reminder for the group. You may copy the summary provided on page 66 or a summary the group comes up with.

2. Large group discussion. Ask group members to volunteer their ideas about why it is difficult to interrupt prejudice or verbal abuse. (For example, racist or prejudiced "jokes" and offhand remarks may be hard to interrupt because the moment passes quickly and you may not want to make a big deal out of it.) Reassure group members that interrupting prejudice is not easy—it takes courage and carefully chosen words to respond in a way that's effective without hurting the other person.

Point out the three possible responses to a situation of prejudice or verbal abuse:

1. Avoidance: Clamming up or ignoring it
2. Aggression: Attacking back
3. Assertion: Confronting in a clear and open way

Tell the group: *Assertion is a healthy expression of emotion, and is an effective way to nonviolently interrupt prejudice and verbal abuse.*

People can respond with assertion to stick up for themselves or to be an ally to someone else. An ally acts by standing up to help someone in a nonviolent and nonconfrontational way. Standing up to acts of prejudice, discrimination, and verbal abuse is difficult, yet necessary in order to create an environment where everyone can feel safe.

3. **Handout.** Distribute the handout, Six Ways to Interrupt Prejudice and Verbal Abuse, and read through the six ways with your group. You may ask volunteers to take turns reading ways.

   Then tell the group: *When you interrupt prejudice or verbal abuse, remember to:*

   - *maintain a calm, controlled tone of voice and a positive tone*

   - *use strategies from the handout, such as active listening, clarifying questions, and "I-Messages" to keep the other person's defensiveness to a minimum*

   - *use anger reducers to calm down so you can think about the words you want to say (you will not be listened to if you make the other person feel guilty or wrong). Anger reducers are anything you do to help yourself calm down, including breathing slowly, counting to 10, taking a walk, using I-Messages to own your feelings, and removing yourself from the situation.*

4. **Large group discussion.** Conduct a group discussion in which you use the following discussion questions:

   - *Which conflict style or styles did Rana use?*

   - *Were there other ways she could have reacted? What are some examples?* (If the group has trouble coming up with ideas, you might start by saying: *Rana could have said, "I feel upset when I hear generalizations made about any group of people. I would appreciate it if you kept them to yourself."*)

Closing: Checking Out What We've Learned

Popcorn-style sharing. Form a large circle with the group and explain how popcorn-style sharing works: everyone may share their thoughts at any time, and there is no pressure to participate. (See page 135 for a complete description of popcorn-style sharing.) Ask for volunteers to share responses to the following questions:

- *What new thoughts or insights emerged from this experience today?*

- *How might you use this experience in your daily life?*

Assign a story from *The Courage to Be Yourself* to be read for your group's next meeting.

Session extension

The following activity can be incorporated into the previous session, if time permits, or can be conducted at the following meeting as a separate session.

Activity: Role-Plays on Interrupting Prejudice and Verbal Abuse

1. **Handouts.** Refer group members to the handout, Six Ways to Interrupt Prejudice and Verbal Abuse. For each guideline, ask group members to brainstorm a few additional starters to help them interrupt prejudice and verbal abuse.

2. **Role-plays.** Ask for three pairs of volunteers to act out role-plays based on Rana's story. In each pair, one person should play Rana, and the other person should play a classmate attacking all Arabs for what happened on September 11, 2001. (See page 135 for a complete description of role-plays.)

- In the first role-play, Rana responds with avoidance, by clamming up or ignoring the attack.

- In the second role-play, Rana responds with aggression, by attacking back (the group member playing Rana can use different words than Rana used in the actual story).

- In the third role-play, Rana responds by being assertive, confronting her classmate in a clear, open way by following the guidelines on the handout.

3. **Large group discussion.** Discuss the groups' reactions after each role-play.

SIX WAYS TO INTERRUPT PREJUDICE AND VERBAL ABUSE

1. Use I-Messages
Sample starters:

- "I don't feel comfortable when you say that."
- "If you had said that to me, I would feel . . ."
- "I don't like it when . . ."
- "I wouldn't want someone to say/do that to me. I don't think anyone deserves to be treated like that."

2. Provide Accurate Information
Sample starters:

- "Here's what I think I know about the situation . . ."
- "I don't think _____ really behaves that way."

3. Ask Clarifying Questions
Sample starters:

- "Can you tell me why you think that about _____?"
- "What exactly do you mean by that?"
- "Why does this upset you so much?"

Continued ⟶

4. Rephrase and Reflect

Sample starters:

- "This is what I heard you say: _____. Is that the way you meant it?" (If the discriminator uses a slur, don't repeat it. Use a letter to note the word or say "a mean word"; this way you're making it especially clear how derogatory and hurtful you find the remark to be.)
- "I heard you call _____ a pretty strong name. Do you really mean that?"

5. Share Your Perspective

Sample starter:

- "That sounds like an assumption to me. I don't think I know _____ well enough to say that."

6. Say What You Need

Sample starters:

- "Even though I'm not _____, it hurts me to hear that word. Please don't use it again."
- "When I'm around, I'd rather you didn't use words like that. Can you handle that?"

Exploring the Nature of Violence

Gay on the Block, by Jeremiah Spears

Pages 61–65 in *The Courage to Be Yourself*

overview

Story Summary

Jeremiah is teased and assaulted in his neighborhood because he is gay. Jeremiah feels comfortable with himself and doesn't understand why people who don't even know him are compelled to harass him. The harassment wears him down and turns his energy to revenge through violence. When he decides it's time for peace, Jeremiah uses the support of his family and friends to move on.

Materials

- Sheets of newsprint or flip chart paper, and markers
- Handout: Defining Violence

Prep Work

- Make a copy of the Defining Violence handout (page 75) for everyone in your group.
- Put the session's agenda on the board or flip chart (see Preview).

Objectives

Group members will:

- develop a definition of violence
- discuss the causes and effects of violence

Themes

- Personal connections
- Social responsibility

Links to the Academic Curriculum

- Character analysis
- Point of view
- Perspective taking

THE SESSION

Preview

Preview the agenda by telling the group that today you will discuss violence—what it is and how it affects people. To do this you will engage in the activities on this agenda:

Agenda: Exploring the Nature of Violence

Reading: "Gay on the Block"
Gathering: Violence Go-Round
Activity: Defining Violence
- Summary
- Small group work
- Large group discussion
- Handout
Closing: Checking Out What We've Learned

Gathering: Violence Go-Round

Have the group form a large circle. Go around the circle and ask each group member to respond to the following: ***What is one image you think of when you hear the word violence?*** List responses on the board or chart paper. (See page 133 for a complete description of go-rounds.)

Activity: Defining Violence

1. **Summary.** Ask volunteers to summarize "Gay on the Block" in two to three sentences. You may wish to write the story summary on the board or chart paper as a reminder for the group. You may copy the summary provided on page 72 or a summary the group comes up with.

2. **Small group work.** Divide teens into groups of three and distribute a sheet of newsprint or flip chart paper and markers to each group. If the number of members in the group is not divisible by three, make groups of four with the extra group members.

Ask each group to discuss the question *what is violence?* Have each group agree on a definition of violence and write it on their chart paper. Next, ask the groups to create a list of the different acts of violence that happen in the story and put those acts into categories. For example:

- People called Jeremiah "faggot" (verbal abuse)

- Jeremiah hit a guy with a plank (assault)

Tell the group that there are no right or wrong categories: each act of violence can be categorized many ways. Give them about 10 minutes to create their definitions and make their lists.

Next, ask group members to think of other categories of violence they have witnessed or know of (for example, sexual harassment, domestic violence, the oppression of certain groups of people, racism, war, the destruction of the environment). Ask the groups to add these to their original list.

3. **Large group discussion.** Post the lists and compare group members' responses. How are the various definitions alike and different? How are the lists alike and different? Ask the group as a whole: ***How do you know when you are seeing or experiencing an act of violence?***

4. **Handout.** Distribute the handout, Defining Violence, and read it together. Compare the handout with the lists made by the groups. Is the handout's definition broader than the groups' definitions? Did the groups' lists of types of violence cover all the types the handout names? How could the groups' lists be expanded in light of the handout's definition of violence? Do group members agree with the definition on the handout?

Closing: Checking Out What We've Learned

Popcorn-style sharing. Form a large circle with the group and explain how popcorn-style sharing works: everyone may share their thoughts at any time, and there is no pressure to participate. (See page 135 for a complete description of popcorn-style sharing.)

Prompt the group by pointing out how much violence we all witness daily: in the news and other media, and sometimes in our schools and community. Then ask: *Let's think peace—what is one important quality of someone you know who acts as a peacemaker or good ally, interrupting violence in their lives or the lives of others?* Give group members a few minutes to respond. Post their responses on the board or chart paper.

Assign a story from *The Courage to Be Yourself* to be read for your group's next meeting.

SESSION EXTENSION

This activity can be incorporated into the previous session, if time permits, or can be conducted at the following meeting as a separate session.

Activity: The Nature of Violence

1. Microlab. Have teens remain in their small groups or, if conducting this extension at a separate meeting, have them break into groups of three (if the number of members in the group is not divisible by three, make groups of four with the extra group members). This microlab is a timed speaking and listening activity in which group members practice good listening skills. (See page 134 for a complete description of microlabs.)

Explain that each person will have one minute to talk to the other people in the group, answering a question you will read out loud. When one person is speaking, the others are only to listen, giving the speaker their full attention—absolutely no interruptions.

Ask the first set of questions listed below. Keep time for the groups and let them know when one minute has passed. At that time, the next person in the group takes a turn to answer the same questions. When everyone in the group has had a turn, repeat the process with each subsequent set of questions.

Questions:

- *Think about the earliest personal encounter with violence you can remember. What happened? How did it change your view of yourself, other people, and the world?*

- *Is it ever okay to hurt another person physically? Where do you draw the line?*

- *Do you believe that people are naturally violent? Why or why not?*

- *How does violence affect how you live? How does it influence the choices you make?*

2. Large group discussion. After the microlab is finished, ask for volunteers to share their answers to each question with the whole group by asking the questions in the order they were introduced and eliciting two or three responses per question.

DeFINING VIOLeNCe

> **Violence:** intentionally trying to injure, demean, threaten, or take advantage of someone. Violence can include physical, verbal, symbolic, and psychological acts. Every act of violence is an expression of aggression.

Direct and Indirect Violence

Direct violence. Includes the most familiar and obvious types of violence, such as war, fist-fights, assault, murder, sexual assault, rape, and domestic abuse. Types of direct violence are:

- **Physical violence.** Acts of aggression that include anything from one person pushing or hitting another to a war between groups of people. Physical violence may occur between strangers or among people who know each other, including family members. Weapons may or may not be involved.

- **Psychological violence.** Teasing, name-calling, telling offensive jokes, verbal threats, or intimidation through gestures or email/instant messaging.

Indirect violence. Not all violent acts are direct; violence can also be present in institutions and communities. When power is concentrated within a corrupt government or organization, it can create extreme inequalities. Some people's needs are comfortably met, while the needs of others are not. When institutionalized power is used to deprive individuals and groups of basic needs and rights, that's violence. Other types of indirect violence are:

- **Bigotry.** Communicating or acting on a belief certain people are inferior or worthless because of their race, ethnicity, religious affiliation, or national identity.

- **Symbolic violence.** Acts that evoke fear and hostility, such as mean or intimidating graffiti.

- **Community violence.** Continued exposure to the use of guns, knives, drugs, and random acts of physical violence. (source: www.ncptsd.va.gov/facts)

- **Social aggression.** Gossiping, spreading cruel rumors, and encouraging others to reject or exclude someone.

- **Passive acceptance of violence.** Standing by and doing nothing when people are being harmed.

Session 14

The Power of Cliques

Nasty Girls, by Alice Wong

Pages 67–71 in *The Courage to Be Yourself*

overview

Story Summary

Alice is uncomfortable because her clique of friends makes fun of others. She discovers that it's more important to be true to her principles than to fit in with the popular crowd.

Materials

- Journals
- Masking tape
- Paper and markers for signs

Prep Work

- Make three signs labeled Strongly Agree, Strongly Disagree, and Not Sure.
- Put the session's agenda on the board or flip chart (see Preview).

Objectives

Group members will:

- explore their feelings about cliques
- write about their experiences with standing up to a group
- discuss how cliques and social power affect their daily lives

Themes

- Cliques and social power
- Exclusion

Links to the Academic Curriculum

- Writing
- Oral expression
- Cooperative listening

THe session

Preview

Preview the agenda by telling the group that today you will discuss how cliques affect everyone. To do this, you will engage in the activities on this agenda:

Agenda: The Power of Cliques

Reading: "Nasty Girls"
Gathering: Clique Opinion Continuum
Activity: Group Maintenance
- Summary
- Journals
- Microlab
- Large group discussion
Closing: Checking Out What We've Learned

Gathering: Clique Opinion Continuum

Make a line with masking tape across the floor of the room (or draw a line across your board). At one end, place a Strongly Agree sign. Label the other end with a Strongly Disagree sign and the middle Not Sure. You could also use two objects on opposite ends of the room to stand as symbols of each end of the spectrum. (See page 134 for a complete description of opinion continuums.)

Ask everyone in the group to stand up. Read the first of the following statements, then ask group members to position themselves along the line to show how they feel about the statement. After group members are in position, ask for volunteers to explain why they are standing where they are. Repeat the process for the second and third statements.

Statements:

1. *I belong to a clique.*
2. *Belonging to a clique or group is important to me.*
3. *I find it uncomfortable to disagree with members of my clique or group, or with close friends.*

Activity: Group Maintenance

1. **Summary.** Ask for volunteers to summarize "Nasty Girls" in two to three sentences. You may wish to write the story summary on the board or chart paper as a reminder for the group. You may copy the summary provided on page 76 or a summary the group comes up with.

2. **Journals.** Ask group members to respond in their journals to the following two sets of questions. (See page 134 for a complete description of journaling.) Read the first set of questions and allow two minutes for group members to respond before reading the next.

   Questions:

   - *Write about a time when you went against what people in a group thought or did. How did people react? How did you feel afterwards?*

   - *Write about a time you didn't go against the crowd, but wished you did. What stopped you from speaking up at the time? What do you wish you had done differently?*

3. **Microlab.** Divide teens into groups of three for a microlab (if the number of members

in the group is not divisible by three, make groups of four with the extra group members). This is a timed speaking and listening activity in which group members practice good listening skills. (See page 134 for a complete description of microlabs.)

Explain that each person will have about one minute to talk to the other people in the group, answering a question you will read out loud. When one person is speaking, the others are only to listen, giving the speaker their full attention—no interruptions.

Ask the first set of questions listed below. Keep time for the group and let group members know when one minute has passed. At that time, the next person in the group should answer the same questions. When everyone in the group has had a turn, go through the same process with each subsequent question.

Questions:

- *Is it natural for people to form groups of friends or cliques? What are the benefits of belonging to a clique? How do cliques offer "social security"?*

- *Why is it important to exclude others to maintain a clique's status?*

- *Alice writes about how being in a clique made her "naïve and close-minded to new people." What are other examples of how cliques hold people back or constrict a true sense of self?*

4. **Large group discussion.** Read the following paragraph from the end of "Nasty Girls": *"I still feel guilty for the years I was a friend to those girls. Even though I didn't do most of the mean things they did, I continued to be a part of their group."* Ask the group if they think Alice should feel guilty or responsible about the way her friends treated others and lead a discussion about cliques and social power. You may come up with your own direction or choose from the following prompts:

- *Even if Alice didn't make rude comments about people or laugh when her friends did, do you think she supported their nastiness?*

- *Why do you think Alice's clique felt so threatened when she befriended new people?*

- *What do you think it means to be popular? How is popularity powerful in high school? Do you think the same is true for life after high school?*

Closing: Checking Out What We've Learned

Ask the group to take out their journals and write their reflections of today's session. Ask the group: *Do you feel like everyone in the group could be honest in their responses about cliques and exclusion? Why are these issues hard to talk about?*

Assign a story from *The Courage to Be Yourself* to be read for your group's next meeting.

Racial and Ethnic Identity

Sticks and Stones, by Yen Yam

Pages 73–77 in The Courage to Be Yourself

overview

Story Summary

Yen describes the insults and attacks she has suffered as a Chinese American living in the United States. She feels conflicted over which culture she belongs to and doesn't feel like she really fits in anywhere. But over time, Yen grows more comfortable with who she is.

Materials

- A soft ball, such as a sponge ball
- Journals
- Pens and paper

Prep Work

- Put the session's agenda on the board or flip chart (see Preview).

Objectives

Group members will:

- discuss how issues surrounding racial and ethnic identity can lead to conflict
- discuss the motives behind discrimination and racism
- share any strategies they have learned for interrupting prejudice and discrimination
- share stories of being allies for others

Themes

- Point of view and perspective taking

Links to the Academic Curriculum

- Literacy: writing and oral expression

THE SESSION

Preview

Preview the agenda by telling the group that today you will discuss how attitudes toward racial and ethnic identity contribute to violence. To do this, you will engage in the activities on this agenda:

Agenda: Racial and Ethnic Identity

Reading: "Sticks and Stones"
Gathering: Ball Toss
Activity: Exploring Racism
  • Summary
  • Journals
  • Small group discussion
  • Large group discussion
Closing: Checking Out What We've Learned

Gathering: Ball Toss

Have the group sit in a circle and ask group members to think about what makes them proud to be a member of their ethnic group. Then say: ***I am proud of being a member of my ethnic group because _____,*** and complete the sentence. This will help group members think about how to respond, create safety, and frame the discussion. Toss the ball to a member of the group and ask her or him to repeat the sentence stem and finish it. That person then tosses the ball to another group member. Repeat the process until everyone in the group has had a chance to complete the sentence or pass.

Activity: Exploring Racism

1. Summary. Ask for volunteers to summarize "Sticks and Stones" in two to three sentences. You may wish to write the story summary on the board or chart paper as a reminder for the group. You may copy the summary provided on page 79 or a summary the group comes up with.

2. Journals. Give the group three minutes to respond to the following question in their journals. Remind them to keep writing the whole time. (See page 134 for a complete description of journaling.) Journal prompt: ***Have you ever felt like an outsider or, as Yen says, "cursed," because of the racial or ethnic group you belong to? Why did you feel that way? Did the feeling eventually change?***

3. Small group discussion. Divide teens into groups of three or four for a dialogue on racism. Explain that in this activity, each group will have three minutes to discuss a set of questions and come up with an answer they agree on. They'll later present their answer to the larger group. They may want to appoint one person to take notes and someone else to act as the speaker when it's time to report to the larger group.

Ask the first set of questions listed below. Keep time for the group and let group members know when three minutes have passed. Then ask each group to summarize their discussion and final answer. Encourage them to mention any parts that were difficult to agree on or any that were particularly easy to agree on.

Ask the second set of questions that follows, again allowing three minutes for the groups to discuss and come up with an answer. When time is up, ask each group to summarize their discussion and final answer.

Questions:

• ***Yen says that racism comes from ignorance. What does she mean? Do you agree? Where do you think it comes from?***

- *Do you agree with Yen that the African Americans who teased her should have known better? Why do you think people who are discriminated against can discriminate against others?*

4. **Large group discussion.** Conduct a discussion based on the following discussion question: *What can an individual do to prevent or interrupt prejudice and racist behavior?*

Closing: Checking Out What We've Learned

In a go-round, ask students to complete each of the following sentence stems (see page 133 for a complete description of go-rounds):

- *I can find the courage to resist racism by _____.*

- *It is really difficult to stand up to racism or discrimination because _____.*

Assign a story from *The Courage to Be Yourself* to be read for your group's next meeting.

Understanding Power—Who Has It? Who Doesn't?

Beating the Bullies, by Miguel Ayala

Pages 79–83 in *The Courage to Be Yourself*

overview

Story Summary

Growing up in a violent, abusive home, Miguel learned to take out his rage on others. Several programs have helped him improve, and he's working hard to get a grip on his emotions.

Materials

- 5" x 8" note cards

Prep Work

- Put the session's agenda on the board or flip chart (see Preview).

Objectives

Group members will:
- identify qualities and attributes of people they think are powerful

- explore the effects of power imbalances on individuals and communities

Themes

- Appreciation for diversity
- Social responsibility
- Anger management and emotional literacy

Links to the Academic Curriculum

- Character education: personal responsibility, integrity, and respect
- Cooperative group learning
- Written expression
- Public speaking

THE SESSION

Preview

Preview the agenda by telling the group that today you will discuss how power is related to anger. To do this, you will engage in the activities on this agenda:

Agenda: Understanding Power—Who Has It? Who Doesn't?

Reading: "Beating the Bullies"
Gathering: What Makes Someone Powerful?
Activity 1: Miguel and Power
- Summary
- Pair share
- Large group discussion
Activity 2: The Community and Power
- Brainstorming
- Pair share
- Large group discussion
Closing: Checking Out What We've Learned

Gathering: What Makes Someone Powerful?

Go-round. Have the group form a large circle. Go around the circle and ask each group member to suggest one idea about what makes someone powerful. (See page 133 for a complete description of go-rounds.) Ideas can be personal qualities or attributes that contribute to a person's power as well as situations that create power for one person over another. If group members have trouble coming up with ideas, you might suggest a couple to get them going, such as, "being someone's manager or teacher," "being physically strong," "being intelligent," "having money," "having responsibility," or "being bigger than someone else."

Activity 1: Miguel and Power

1. **Summary.** Ask for volunteers to summarize "Beating the Bullies" in two to three sentences. You may wish to write the story summary on the board or chart paper as a reminder for the group. You may copy the summary provided on page 82 or a summary the group comes up with.

2. **Pair share.** Divide the group into pairs and ask the first of the following questions. (See page 135 for a complete description of pair shares.) Allow the pairs to have a dialogue on the question for two minutes, then ask for volunteers to share what they discussed with the larger group. After a few pairs have shared with the larger group, ask the next set of questions and allow the pairs to have a dialogue about it. Again, ask for volunteers to share what they talked about when the time is up. Repeat the process for the third set of questions.

   Questions:

   - *How do parents have power over their children?*

   - *In what ways did Miguel's mother misuse her power? What do you think was the worst thing she did?*

   - *From the way his mother treated him, what did Miguel learn about power? How does he use power?*

3. **Large group discussion.** Conduct a large group discussion based on the following discussion points:

   - *Miguel felt powerless and, at times, hopeless. Besides being mistreated by his family, what other circumstances may have made Miguel feel this way?*

- *How can feelings of powerlessness and hopelessness lead to violence?*

Activity 2: The Community and Power

1. Brainstorming. Divide the group into new pairs (with a different partner than in the earlier pair share) and pass out a 5" x 8" note card to each pair. Have the pairs write "More Powerful Groups" on the left side of their card and "Less Powerful Groups" on the right side. Ask them to make a list on the left side of people, groups, and institutions in their community that have power. Then ask them to brainstorm a list on the right side of the card of less powerful groups that are related in some way to the people, groups, and institutions on the left side. For example: a more powerful group might be doctors and a less powerful group related to doctors might be patients. (See page 133 for a complete description of brainstorming.)

2. Pair share. With the group still in pairs, ask the first of the following questions. (See page 135 for a complete description of pair shares.) Allow the pairs to have a dialogue on the question for two minutes, then ask for volunteers to share what they discussed with the larger group. After a few pairs have shared with the larger group, ask the next questions and allow the pairs to

have a dialogue about them. Again, ask for volunteers to share what they talked about when the time is up.

Questions:

- *How would you describe the people and groups who have more power and those who have less?*

- *What differences do you notice when you compare the two lists? What's something that stands out for you when you compare the lists?*

3. Large group discussion. Conduct a large group discussion around the following questions:

- *What is the relationship between power and*
   the choices a person has?
   the resources a person has access to?
   who's safe?

- *Does power give people more choices, resources, and safety? Or do those things give a person power?*

Closing: Checking Out What We've Learned

Ask the group to share one thing they've learned about power from this lesson. You may prompt them by asking: *How does unequal power among different groups affect you? How does it affect everyone?*

Assign a story from *The Courage to Be Yourself* to be read for your group's next meeting.

Exploring the Nature of Conflict

It Ain't Easy Being Hard, by Danny Ticali

Pages 85–87 in *The Courage to Be Yourself*

overview

Story Summary

Danny enjoyed beating up people and feeling tough. Over time, he begins to understand the consequences of his actions and decides to turn his back on violence.

Materials

- Handout: Conflict Survey

Prep Work

- Cut several pieces of construction paper (various colors) into 3" x 3" squares. Make sure there are plenty of blue, black, and red pieces, which are the most commonly chosen (see Gathering).

- Make a copy of the Conflict Survey handout (page 88) for each member of your group.

- Put the session's agenda on the board or flip chart (see Preview).

Objectives

Group members will:

- define conflict and violence
- distinguish between conflict and violence
- identify what's positive about conflict
- analyze a conflict they have experienced

Themes

- Managing and resolving conflict
- Analyzing the nature of conflict

Links to the Academic Curriculum

- Critical thinking
- Cooperative group work
- Written and verbal expression

THE SESSION

Preview

Preview the agenda by telling the group that today you will discuss the differences between conflict and violence, and look at the positive aspects of conflict. To do this, you will engage in the activities on this agenda:

Agenda: Exploring the Nature of Conflict

Reading: "It Ain't Easy Being Hard"
Gathering: If Conflict Were a Color
Activity 1: What Is Conflict?
  • Summary
  • Conflict web
  • Large group discussion
Activity 2: What's Positive About Conflict?
  • Large group discussion
  • Brainstorming
Closing: Checking Out What We've Learned

Gathering: If Conflict Were a Color

Say to students: *If conflict were a color, what color would it be?* Pass the stack or basket of colored squares and allow the group members to choose the color of construction paper that represents conflict to them.

When everyone has chosen, ask for volunteers to talk about why they chose the color they did.

Activity 1: What Is Conflict?

1. Summary. Ask for volunteers to summarize "It Ain't Easy Being Hard" in two to three sentences. You may wish to write the story summary on the board or chart paper as a reminder for the group. You may copy the summary provided on page 85 or a summary the group comes up with.

2. Conflict web. Write "Conflict" in the center of the board or chart paper and circle it. Ask group members to suggest words and ideas that they associate with that word. Add the group members' associated words to the board with a line stemming out from the word in the center. To visually connect various aspects of the key concept and the following associations, you can cluster related ideas together. (See page 136 for a complete description of concept webbing/ concept maps.)

3. Large group discussion. Conduct a group discussion using the following discussion questions:

  • *What do you notice about the web?*

  • *Are there any generalizations we might make about our associations?*

  • *Why are most of our associations negative?*

Activity 2: What's Positive About Conflict?

1. Large group discussion. Tell the group that many people associate conflict with violence. As a group, come up with an explanation of the difference between conflict and violence. Then compare your group's explanation with the following discussion points:

  • *Conflict is normal and natural and not always avoidable.*

  • *Conflict does not always lead to violence.*

  • *Violence is rooted in conflict.*

  • *A person's reaction to conflict determines whether violence occurs.*

Continue the discussion by pointing out that every time we encounter another person (such as a family member, classmate, teacher, friend, or stranger) there is potential for conflict. Everyone has their own unique ideas about how things should happen, how they want to be treated, and what they find appropriate or rude in any given situation. However, conflict is not wholly negative—it is often an opportunity for growth. Ask group members:

- *Was there ever a time you dreaded a conflict/confrontation and it turned out to be a positive experience?*

- *Can you think of something you learned from a personal conflict?*

- *What is hard about working together to solve conflicts? What makes it worth the effort?*

2. **Brainstorming.** Ask group members to brainstorm a list of things that were positive about conflict in Danny's story. (See page 133 for a complete description of brainstorming.) Some positive examples are:

- It brought him closer to the kid he protected.

- It helped shake up Danny's thinking so that he eventually had new ways of looking at things.

Emphasize this last point. The violence in Danny's past is inexusable, but his experiences with violence forced him to examine what kind of person he had become. He realized that he didn't like being someone everyone was afraid of. He wanted to live a more positive life.

Close the discussion by telling group members that although conflict is inevitable, they control their attitudes toward conflict and they can choose to respond positively to the conflicts they face.

Closing: Checking Out What We've Learned

Handout. Distribute the handout, Conflict Survey, and ask group members to fill it out. Let them know that you are the only person who will see their survey, and that in order to get the most out of the exercise they should be as honest as possible.

Assign a story from *The Courage to Be Yourself* to be read for your group's next meeting.

CONFLICT SURVey

‖‣ **Most people fight or argue over** _____

_____ .

‖‣ **People generally respond to conflicts by** _____

_____ .

‖‣ **I fight or argue when** _____

_____ .

‖‣ **I get upset or angry when other people** _____

_____ .

‖‣ **I make others angry when I** _____

_____ .

‖‣ **When I'm talking to someone who is really angry or upset, the most important thing for me to do is** _____

_____ .

‖‣ **When I'm really angry or upset with someone, the most important thing for me to do is** _____

_____ .

‖‣ **When I'm upset at, mad at, or bothered by another person, I can** _____

_____ .

‖‣ **When I have a disagreement or conflict with someone, we can agree to** _____

_____ .

Overcoming Preconceptions and Stereotypes (Part 1)

At Home in the Projects, by Fabiola Duvalsaint

Pages 89–92 in *The Courage to Be Yourself*

Note: This session deals with classism and commonly held stereotypes about the violence, drugs, and poverty associated with living in a housing development or "the projects." This issue may be sensitive for some group members. You may want to remind the group that they always have the right to pass on talking if they want to.

overview

Story Summary

Fabiola associates the housing projects with crime and violence and is surprised to have befriended someone who lives there. At first she's afraid to go to her friend's house, but when she does, she learns that her fears are unfounded—she feels safe and her friend's family is much like her own.

Materials

- Journals

Prep Work

- Put the session's agenda on the board or flip chart (see Preview).

Objectives

Group members will:

- discuss the role of fear in perpetrating stereotypes and misconceptions about others
- discuss how they've been feared or stereotyped based on group, gender, race, ability, or national origin
- discuss preconceptions or stereotypes they've had about others

Themes

- Point of view and perspective taking
- Appreciation for diversity

Links to the Academic Curriculum

- Verbal and written expression
- Literary perspective taking
- Critical thinking
- Cooperative group work

THE SESSION

Preview

Preview the agenda by telling the group that today you will discuss how fear contributes to stereotypes and conflict. To do this you will engage in the activities on this agenda:

Agenda: Overcoming Preconceptions and Stereotypes

Reading: "At Home in the Projects"
Gathering: They Think I Am
Activity: Fears of Difference
  • Summary
  • Journals
  • Pair share
  • Large group discussion
Closing: Checking Out What We've Learned

Gathering: They Think I Am

Have the group sit in a circle (if there's room) and go around the circle asking each group member to complete the following sentence stem: "Before people get to know me well, they think I am _____."

Activity: Fears of Difference

1. **Summary.** Ask volunteers to summarize "At Home in the Projects" in two to three sentences. You may wish to write the story summary on the board or chart paper as a reminder for the group. You may copy the summary provided on page 89 or a summary the group comes up with.

2. **Journals.** Read the first of the following sets of questions and ask group members to respond in their journals. (See page 134

for a complete description of journaling.) Allow two minutes for group members to write, then read the next set.

   Questions:

   • *Did you ever have a fear of a person, a group of people, or a place, based on a stereotype or prejudice? Did you get over that fear? Why or why not?*

   • *Has anyone ever been mistrustful or afraid of you? Why were they afraid and how did that make you feel?*

   Ask volunteers to share what they wrote or talk about fears of difference in a general way. Lead a group discussion of the responses.

3. **Pair share.** Have students partner up for a pair share, then read aloud the first of the following discussion questions. (See page 135 for a complete description of pair-shares.) Allow one minute for one partner in each pair to answer the question, while the other partner listens. When the minute is up, have the second partner respond for one minute while the first listens. After the second minute is up, read the second set of questions and allow another two minutes— one for each partner in each pair—for responses. Repeat again for the third set of questions.

   Questions:

   • *Where do stereotypes come from?*

   • *How do stereotypes affect those being stereotyped? How do they affect those who believe in the stereotype?*

   • *Is there such a thing as a good stereotype? Why or why not?*

4. **Large group discussion.** Ask the questions in the order they were introduced, and elicit two or three responses per question from volunteers. Pay attention to the ways answers are similar to and different from each other. Use responses as a jumping-off point for a larger discussion of stereotypes. If you feel comfortable doing so, relating a personal anecdote about your experience with stereotypes can help create a dynamic discussion.

Closing: Checking Out What We've Learned

Ask group members what thoughts or behaviors they would like to say good-bye to and what new thoughts or behaviors they would welcome. Then, in a go-round, ask each group member to say, "Good-bye _____, hello _____," filling in the blanks. You can begin the activity by going first. (See page 133 for a complete description of go-rounds.)

Assign a story from *The Courage to Be Yourself* to be read for your group's next meeting.

Responding to Conflict—What Do We Do? (Part 2)

My Secret Love, Anonymous

Pages 93–96 in *The Courage to Be Yourself*

overview

Story Summary

The author is a tough-talking, tough-walking dude who has to keep his love of *The Sound of Music*, *West Side Story*, and other musicals a secret for fear of being humiliated by his rap-loving peers.

Materials

- Handout: Six Conflict Resolution Styles
- Journals

Prep Work

- If you haven't done Session 9, make a copy of the Six Conflict Resolution Styles handout for everyone in the group (pages 56–57).
- Put the session's agenda on the board or flip chart (see Preview).

Objectives

Group members will:

- reflect on different approaches to conflict, particularly internal conflict
- identify the dominant style they use in responding to external and internal conflict

Themes

- Managing and resolving conflict
- Conflict analysis

Links to the Academic Curriculum

- Verbal expression
- Writing
- Critical thinking

THE SESSION

Preview

Preview the agenda by telling the group that today you will discuss different styles of responding to conflict, especially internal conflict. To do this you will engage in the activities on this agenda:

Agenda: Responding to Conflict—What Do We Do?

Reading: "My Secret Love"
Gathering: Conflict Go-Round
Activity 1: Identifying the Six Conflict
   Resolution Styles
   • Summary
   • Large group discussion
   • Handout
   • Journals
Activity 2: Identifying Personal Conflict
   Resolution Styles
   • Microlab
Closing: Checking Out What We've Learned

Gathering: Conflict Go-Round

Sit in a circle (if you have room) and do a go-round, asking each member of your group to complete the following sentence: "When I have a conflict, I usually _____." (See page 133 for a complete description of go-rounds.)

Activity 1: Identifying the Six Conflict Resolution Styles

1. Summary. Ask volunteers to summarize "My Secret Love" in two to three sentences. You may wish to write the story summary on the board or chart paper as a reminder for the group. You may copy the summary provided on page 92 or a summary the group comes up with.

2. Large group discussion. Discuss with the group the fact that the author goes through a conflict, though some might not think of it as a typical conflict because it does not lead to violence and only involves one person—the author. Tell the group: *A conflict is when two people, groups, or ideas compete or struggle against each other. For example, two people might argue or fight over what music to listen to in the car. In an internal conflict, the two things that are struggling against each other are thoughts or ideas in one person's mind. The writer of this story has an internal conflict about whether to reveal his love for musicals to his peers. He has two needs: to be true to himself and what he loves, and to be accepted by his peers.*

Ask the group: *Why is this conflict so hard for the writer? What do you think of the way the author responds to the conflict?*

Emphasize to the group that conflict itself is not necessarily good or bad. It's a person's response to conflict that usually determines how it is resolved.

3. Handout. If you have done Session 9: Responding to Conflict—What Do We Do? (Part 1), briefly review the Six Conflict Resolution Styles handout from that session to refresh group members' memories. If you have not done Session 9, distribute the handout (pages 56–57) and ask for a volunteer to read each style description aloud to the group. After each style is read, ask group members to suggest the strengths and weaknesses of that style. Emphasize the fact that because each conflict resolution style has its strengths and weaknesses, the important thing is to recognize that there are different methods of dealing with conflict and that each person can choose the method that is right for each situation.

Discuss with the group how these conflict resolution styles can be used with internal conflicts. For example, in Directing/Controlling, you may have a conflict in which you force yourself to do what's "right," even though it may feel better or be easier or more fun to do something else—like standing up for a target of bullying even when you know you may be ostracized for it. If you are comfortable doing so, it can be helpful to volunteer a personal anecdote as an example. Encourage group members to suggest examples, either real to life or in the abstract.

4. **Journals.** Have students write in their journals for five minutes about an internal conflict they've had and how they handled it. (See page 134 for a complete description of journaling.) Ask: ***Did you use one of the conflict resolution styles? Would another style have worked better?***

Activity 2: Identifying Personal Conflict Resolution Styles

Microlab. Break into groups of three for a microlab (if the number of members in the group is not divisible by three, make groups of four with the extra group members). This is a timed speaking and listening activity in which group members practice good listening skills. (See page 134 for a complete description of microlabs.)

Explain that each person will have about one minute to talk to the other people in the group, answering a question you will read out loud. When one person is speaking, the others are only to listen, giving the speaker their full attention—no interruptions.

Ask the first set of questions listed below. Keep time for the group and let them know when one minute has passed. At that time, the next person in the group should answer the same question. When all the people in the group have had their turns, go through the same process with each subsequent set of questions.

Questions:

- ***What conflict resolution style do you use most often when you have a conflict with others? How well does it work for you?***

- ***Can you use the same conflict resolution style or styles when you have an internal conflict? Why or why not?***

- ***Are there any styles you never use? If so, why don't you use them?***

Closing: Checking Out What We've Learned

Ask volunteers to complete the following sentence, written on the board or chart paper: ***My dominant conflict resolution style is _____, but I can see using _____ style because _____.***

Assign a story from *The Courage to Be Yourself* to be read for your group's next meeting.

All About Anger

My Group Home Scapegoat, by Angela Rutman

Pages 97–99 in *The Courage to Be Yourself*

overview

Story Summary

Angela witnesses her fellow group home residents taking out their anger on another girl. She has done it herself in the past, but vows to stick up for the girl the next time it happens.

Materials

- A soft ball
- Flip chart paper and markers
- Handout: Anger Makes You Lose Your Head
- For extension: 5" x 8" note cards and Anger Reducers handout

Prep Work

- Decide how you want to use this session. Anger is such an important topic in conflict resolution that this session includes three extensions, which can be used to extend the following session if time permits or to conduct additional sessions on separate days.
- If you feel comfortable sharing a personal story with your group, think of a time when you were overwhelmed with anger and said or did something you later regretted. Think about what caused your feelings, how you reacted, what you wish you would have done differently, and how you learned from the experience. (You will use this story to prompt discussion in Activity 2: Anger Makes You Lose Your Head.)
- Make a copy of the handouts, Anger Makes You Lose Your Head (page 101) and Anger Reducers (page 102), for everyone in your group.
- Put the session's agenda on the board or flip chart (see Preview).

Objectives

Group members will:

- explore what makes them angry
- become more aware of their personal anger cues, triggers, and reducers
- examine their responses to anger and explore alternative responses

Themes

- Emotional literacy
- Managing and resolving conflict
- Perspective taking and point of view

Links to the Academic Curriculum

- Verbal expression
- Cooperative learning

THE SESSION

Preview

Preview the agenda by telling the group that today you will discuss what makes people angry and how they can deal with anger in positive and constructive ways when it comes up. To do this you will engage in the activities on this agenda:

Agenda: All About Anger

Reading: "My Group Home Scapegoat"
Gathering: Anger Ball Toss
Activity 1: Anger Triggers
  • Summary
  • Brainstorm
  • Pair share
  • Large group discussion
Activity 2: Anger Makes You Lose Your Head
  • Large group discussion
  • Journals
  • Handouts
Closing: Checking Out What We've Learned

Gathering: Anger Ball Toss

Have the group stand in a circle, with you holding a soft ball (such as a sponge ball). Begin by saying, *I feel angry when* _____ and completing the sentence. Then toss the ball to someone else in the circle. That person also says, "I feel angry when _____," completes the sentence, and tosses the ball to someone else. Continue the process until everyone has the opportunity to share (or pass).

Activity 1: Anger Triggers

1. Summary. Ask volunteers to summarize "My Group Home Scapegoat" in two to three

sentences. You may wish to write the story summary on the board or chart paper as a reminder for the group. You may copy the summary provided on page 95 or a summary the group comes up with.

2. Brainstorm. Write the words *Anger Triggers* on the board or flip chart. Ask the group to brainstorm all the reasons in the story why people (including Angela) took out their anger on Jasmine. (See page 133 for a complete description of brainstorming.) What triggered their anger? Write the answers under the Anger Triggers heading. The list of anger triggers may include:

  • They were angry to begin with and took it out on Jasmine.

  • They felt superior to Jasmine.

  • They felt safer if Jasmine was getting bullied, because it was someone else being mistreated, not them.

  • Being angry at Jasmine made some girls feel part of the group.

  • Kids who were abused and neglected by their families took out their anger on weaker kids like Jasmine.

  • Jasmine seemed weak or had an attitude, so she became a target.

3. Pair share. Have group members partner up. Ask each member of the pair to describe a recent time when he or she became angry. Group members should talk about what happened to make them angry, how they responded, and what the outcome was. (See page 135 for a complete description of pair shares.) Allow two minutes for one partner in each pair to talk, while the other partner listens. When the two minutes are up, have the second partner respond for two minutes while the first listens.

4. **Large group discussion.** Ask for volunteers to share their stories. Encourage them to be specific. Add their contributions to the existing list of anger triggers on the board or flip chart paper. Your group members will probably cite such common causes as:

- when someone hurts, criticizes, or embarrasses me

- when I am denied what I want or need

- when others have behaved in a way that I judge offensive and/or morally wrong

- when I can't control a situation and feel powerless

- when I witness or experience injustice, prejudice, or violence

Activity 2: Anger Makes You Lose Your Head

1. **Large group discussion.** If you feel comfortable doing so, sharing a personal experience about a time you were overwhelmed with anger and said or did something that you later regretted is a great way to open up this discussion. If you don't want to share a personal story, you can speak more generally about the power anger has to take over our emotions. Regardless if you share your own story, emphasize the following points and encourage group members to reflect on their own experiences with anger:

- Sometimes anger blocks out the ability to think clearly. Angry people may feel stuck—paralyzed by their strong feelings and unable to speak or act.

- Sometimes people revisit angry moments time and again in their minds, replaying the situation like a movie—adding things they wish they'd said or done, cutting out the things they want to take back (such as things they said that hurt people).

2. **Journals.** Have group members write for two minutes in their journals about an experience when their feelings of anger led them to behave in ways that had negative consequences. (See page 134 for a complete description of journaling.) When the two minutes are up, ask for volunteers to talk about the experiences they wrote about.

3. **Handout.** Distribute the Anger Makes You Lose Your Head handout and give group members a few minutes to look at it. This illustration can help group members better understand what happens to their bodies when they get angry. Tell the group: ***When something triggers your anger, an adrenaline burst in your body makes it hard to stay calm. After about ten seconds the adrenaline is at its strongest. That's when you're at the most risk of doing something that will make things worse—or that you'll regret later. Remember, you can't control what happens inside your body. Anger is natural and your body's response is natural. But being aware of what's happening to your body—and remembering that you*** will ***calm down—can help you stay in control.***

Use this handout as a starting point for discussing impulsive behavior—the things we say and do without thinking. Remind the group of Angela's story. When Angela realized the reason she was being mean to Jasmine—because of her own anger—she was able to control her anger and make the decision not to hurt Jasmine any more.

The handout also provides an opportunity to discuss the feelings of regret and guilt that we often experience when the adrenaline wears off. This graphic helps group members understand why it's important to learn techniques for managing and controlling anger. Tell the group: **Often, as the release of stress hormones and adrenaline ends, your body feels tired. In addition, you may also feel regret once your ability to reason has returned.**

Closing: Checking Out What We've Learned

Ask for volunteers to respond to the following questions:

- *Are there situations in which anger is a healthy response? If so, what are they?*

- *Are there situations in which anger is counterproductive? If so, what are they?*

Talk to your group about anger as a normal, healthy emotion. We have many choices for how to express and deal with anger. Some people fly off the handle, while other people just dismiss it. Make the distinction between feeling and behavior: anger is a *feeling;* what we choose to do with the feeling is our *behavior.* A behavior may have positive or negative consequences.

Assign a story from *The Courage to Be Yourself* to be read for your group's next meeting.

SESSION EXTENSIONS

These activities can extend the previous session, if time permits, or be conducted at the next meeting to continue examining anger.

Activity 1: More on Anger Triggers

1. **Note cards.** Give each group member a 5" x 8" note card. Have them write "Anger Triggers" at the top of the card and list four or five behaviors, words, or phrases that make them angry.

2. **Pair share.** Divide the group into pairs and ask the first of the following questions. (See page 135 for a complete description of pair shares.) Allow the pairs to have a dialogue on the question for two minutes, then ask for volunteers to share what they discussed with the larger group. After a few pairs have shared with the larger group, ask the next question and allow the pairs to have a dialogue about it. Again, ask for volunteers to share what they talked about when the time is up. Repeat the process for the third question.

   Questions:

   - *How do you know when you're angry? What are the physical cues that let you know you're becoming angry?*

   - *How do you usually react to being angry?*

   - *Do you have a "long fuse" or a "short fuse"?*

   Point out to group members that physical cues of anger can be warning signs to stop and think about what we want to do next.

Activity 2: Responses to Anger and Cooling Off

1. **Brainstorm.** Ask the group to brainstorm a list called Ways People Deal with Their Anger. (See page 133 for a complete description of brainstorming.) Your list can include all ways of dealing with anger, not just constructive ones. Record all ideas on newsprint. Some common responses are:

- Blow off steam: Release angry energy by pounding a pillow, jogging, or finding a place to scream where you won't bother anyone.

- Talk it out with the person you're angry with. Tell that person how you feel and what you want to happen.

- Talk about it to a friend who's not involved.

- Chill out by taking a few deep breaths, counting to 10, listening to music, or just being alone for a few minutes.

- Stuff it in and pretend nothing's wrong.

- Get back at someone verbally through name-calling, sarcasm, put-downs, intimidating, or threatening.

- Pick a fight, start an argument, or destroy someone else's stuff.

- Escape by reading a book, watching TV, eating, playing basketball, or going out with friends.

- Make a joke of the situation and laugh it off.

- Ignore the situation.

- Get aggressive by fighting, hitting, or kicking.

- Stop, think, and ask questions: What just set me off? What do I really want to happen now? Am I willing to look for a solution?

- Tell myself, "I'm in charge of what I do. I can choose what to do right now. I don't want the other person to control what I do or say."

- Keep my voice quiet and calm.

- Say, "I'm too angry to talk now, but I want to talk later."

2. Large group discussion. Conduct a large group discussion about your brainstorm list by using one or a few of the following discussion questions:

- *Which strategies might make the situation worse?*

- *Which strategies might be self-destructive?*

- *Which strategies would give you a chance to stand up for yourself without being abusive or physically aggressive?*

- *Which strategies are hardest for you to use? Easiest?*

- *Which strategies would help you to manage your anger so that you don't lose it and/ or hurt others or yourself? Circle these strategies.*

- *How does Angela claim personal power in dealing with her anger and the anger of others? What does she do in order to control her anger toward Jasmine?*

Activity 3: Responses to Anger Role-Plays

1. Introduction. Explain that a person can respond to anger in one of three ways: suppression, aggression, or assertiveness.

Suppression: Acting as if nothing happened. If somebody insults you, you can pretend you didn't hear it or change the subject.

Aggression: Lashing out with words or physical attack. If someone insults you, you think of a worse insult to throw back, or punch that person in the face.

Assertiveness: Letting the other person know that the insult is unacceptable without attempting to hurt the other person in return.

2. **Role-play.** Ask two group members to role-play a conflict between Jasmine and another group home resident using the following scenario. Tell the actors they should not touch each other or use inappropriate language. (See page 135 for a complete description of role-plays.) Have the rest of the group be observers. Read the scenario:

> *The kids in Angela's group home continue to tease Jasmine. Most of the time, Jasmine tries to ignore it. One day, a kid smacks Jasmine in the back of the head. For Jasmine, it's the last straw. She reacts aggressively.*

Ask the two volunteers to role-play what happens next. Stop the action after about one minute. Ask group members who were performing the role-play to stay in character and say how they are feeling at this point. Then ask the observers how they feel about the conflict.

3. **Brainstorm.** Ask the group to brainstorm ways that Jasmine could handle the situation assertively—that is, with firmness and directness, not suppression or aggression. Write their suggestions on the board.

4. **Alternative role-play.** Once you have several suggestions on your list, ask for two volunteers to choose one and conduct a role-play with a new ending. In this role-play, Jasmine will respond to her anger using that suggestion. Again, stop the action after one minute and ask the players how their characters are feeling and how they themselves are feeling. How did the conflict work out? If you have time, repeat the process using other volunteers and other assertive solutions from the list.

5. **Handout.** Distribute the Anger Reducers handout and ask the group to fill it out. For the top part ("Three things I can do to cool down my anger"), group members can refer to the items on the group's brainstorm list for ideas. Group members should keep their handouts.

ANGER MAKES YOU LOSE YOUR HEAD

Be Aware of How Anger Affects Your Body!

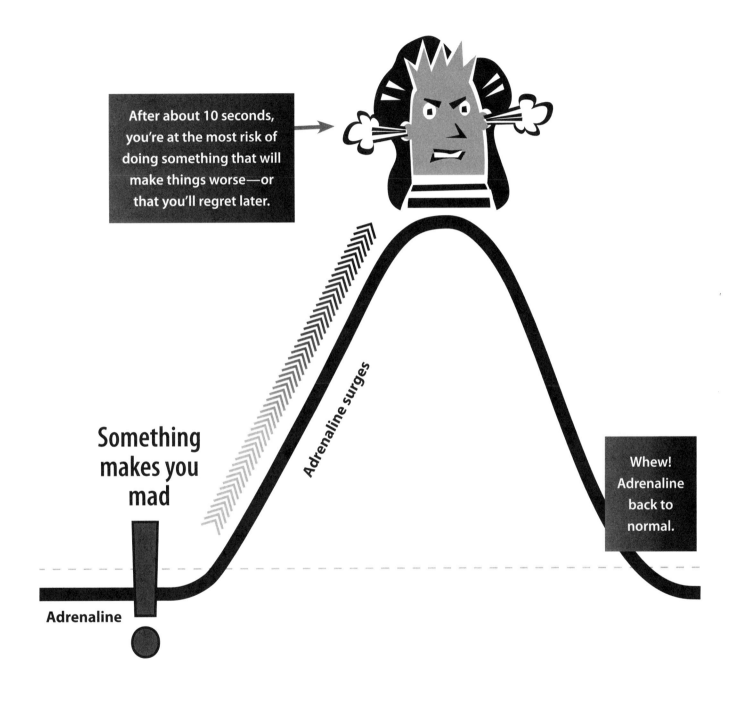

After about 10 seconds, you're at the most risk of doing something that will make things worse—or that you'll regret later.

Adrenaline surges

Something makes you mad

Adrenaline

Whew! Adrenaline back to normal.

ANGer reducers

Three things I can do to cool down my anger:

1. _____

_____

2. _____

_____

3. _____

_____

Things I can say to myself so I don't do something I'll regret in the heat of an angry moment (fill out as many as you can think of):

_____

_____

_____

_____

_____

_____

From Being a Bystander to Taking a Stand

There Are 20 Sides to Every Story, by Stephany Cover

Pages 101–103 in *The Courage to Be Yourself*

overview

Story Summary

A false rumor has Stephany in conflict with Meredith, the school bully. In the end, they resolve the misunderstanding without violence by engaging in mediation and become friends.

Materials

- Flip chart paper or newsprint, and markers

Prep Work

- For Activity 1, create five signs from chart paper using large letters that say Target, Aggressor, Instigator, Bystander, and Ally. Post the signs in five different places in your room. Photocopy the Role Cards handout (page 107) and cut out the cards.

- For Activity 2, write each of the writing prompts on a separate sheet of flip chart paper, leaving plenty of space for group members' answers. You will post them in different parts of the room after Activity 1.

- Put the session's agenda on the board or flip chart (see Preview).

Objectives

Group members will:

- identify what it means to be a target, an aggressor, an instigator, a bystander, or an ally

- share ideas for how they can become allies to others in their school community in ways that prevent prejudice and promote diversity

Themes

- Appreciating diversity
- Social responsibility
- Personal connections

Links to the Academic Curriculum

- Cooperative group work
- Verbal expression and point of view
- Critical thinking and analysis

THE SESSION

Preview

Preview the agenda by telling the group that today you will discuss the way conflicts can be resolved when you change from a bystander into someone who takes a stand and becomes involved in solving the conflict. To do this you will engage in the activities on this agenda:

Agenda: From Being a Bystander to Taking a Stand

Reading: "There Are 20 Sides to Every Story"
Gathering: Diverse Groups
Activity 1: Targets, Aggressors, Instigators, Bystanders, and Allies
  • Summary
  • Discussion points
  • Role cards
  • Large group discussion
Activity 2: Groups at Your School or in Your Neighborhood
  • Prompts
  • Rotation stations
  • Large group discussion
Closing: Checking Out What We've Learned

Gathering: Diverse Groups

Popcorn-Style Sharing. Form a large circle with the group and explain how popcorn-style sharing works: everyone may share their thoughts at any time, and there is no pressure to participate. (See page 135 for a complete description of popcorn-style sharing.) Ask for volunteers to share a time in recent memory when it was safe, fun, or cool to be in a group made up of individuals from very different backgrounds (such as cultural and family background, ethnicity, religion, gender, or groups in school).

Activity 1: Targets, Aggressors, Instigators, Bystanders, and Allies

1. **Summary.** Ask volunteers to summarize "There Are 20 Sides to Every Story" in two to three sentences. You may wish to write the story summary on the board or chart paper as a reminder for the group. You may copy the summary provided on page 103 or a summary the group comes up with.

2. **Discussion points.** If you have done Session 7: Interrupting Bullying and Harassment with your group, you may want to briefly review the five roles a person can play in a harassment situation. If you haven't done that session, introduce the harassment roles:

   Target: A person or group being harassed.

   Aggressor: A person who taunts, threatens, humiliates, victimizes, or physically harms the target. Also known as a bully.

   Instigator: A person who spreads rumors or gossip, or makes things up to encourage others to harass the target. Instigating can be done verbally, on the Internet, through instant messages, or through graffiti in public places.

   Bystander: A person who either witnesses or knows that the target is being harassed and does or says nothing. Bystanders may be adults or even a friend of the target.

Ally: A person who stands up for the target by defending her or him nonviolently and by challenging the aggressor's attacks.

Explain to the group that when people witness a person or group being harassed, they have a choice to make. They can choose to be an instigator (encouraging or adding to the harassment), a bystander (saying or doing nothing to change the situation), or an ally (working with and acting in support of the targeted person or group).

3. **Role cards.** Ask for five volunteers and distribute one of the five role cards (Target, Aggressor, Instigator, Bystander, or Ally) to each. Each card explores the thoughts and feelings of one person who was involved in "There Are 20 Sides to Every Story." Give the volunteers a few seconds to read their cards.

Next, ask the volunteers to stand under the sign they think corresponds with the experience of the person described on their cards. When they have placed themselves by the signs, ask one of them to read his or her card. Ask the group if they agree or disagree with the sign that person is standing under, based on what the person read from the card (i.e., do they agree that the person is an ally, target, or other role), and why or why not. Then rotate from sign to sign, giving each group member an opportunity to read his or her card and asking the group if they agree with the label that person chose. Discuss with the group how the same thoughts, feelings, or situation can indicate a different harassment role to different people.

4. **Large group discussion.** After each volunteer has read, conduct a large group discussion using the following questions:

- *What do you think Stephany wants or needs her allies to do to show their support?*

- *If you were one of Stephany's allies, what would you say to her? What would you do?*

- *A bystander in a harassment situation always has the potential to become an ally to the target. In this story, what would have to change in order for more bystanders to become allies to Stephany? What skills, conditions, or support do you think a bystander would need in order to become comfortable enough to become an ally?*

Talk about how hard it can be to act as an ally in some situations. For example, it's hard to be an ally if you are the only person standing up against an injustice or mean-spirited act. It is also difficult to be an ally if authority figures such as teachers do not support you. Tell the group that it takes courage to be an ally for yourself and others.

Activity 2: Groups at Your School or in Your Neighborhood

1. **Prompts.** Post the following writing prompts, one each on a separate sheet of flip chart paper, in separate spots around the room. Provide a marker at each station.

Note: If your group is not in a school environment, you may change the phrase "at your school" in each question to "in your neighborhood."

Station 1: What are some groups at your school that are targeted by individuals and groups who are more popular, or who have more status and influence? For each group you list, also list one way you could act as an ally to people in that group.

Station 2: What's already happening at your school that helps make all groups feel included and welcomed?

Station 3: At your school, in what classes, activities, projects, and events do you notice the most positive interaction among people from different groups? For each item on your list, also list the reasons why that event attracts a genuine mix of people.

Station 4: At your school, in what classes, activities, projects, and events do group members tend to segregate by group? For each item on your list, also list what you think are reasons that event leads to segregation.

2. **Rotation stations.** Divide teens into four groups and direct one group to stand at each question. Give the groups two minutes to discuss the question at their stations and record their responses below the question on the paper. (See page 135 for a complete description of rotation stations.) Encourage them to try to record two or three responses.

After two minutes, ask the groups to rotate to the right to the next station. Allow them another two minutes to discuss and record their responses to the new question. Rotate two more times, so each group gets a chance to respond to each of the four questions.

3. **Large group discussion.** After the groups have had a chance to respond to all four questions, ask for volunteers to read the answers at their station and discuss the responses.

Closing: Checking Out What We've Learned

Have group members return to their seats and write down one thing they would like to change in their school that would promote diversity, and one thing they can do to become a better ally to targeted groups. Ask for volunteers to share what they wrote.

Assign a story from *The Courage to Be Yourself* to be read for your group's next meeting.

TarGeT, AGGressor, INSTIGATOr, BYSTANDer, AND ALLY CarDS

I'm Stephany. People have spread false rumors about me and now Meredith is angry at me and wants to fight. I haven't done anything to anyone, and now the whole thing is out of control. I'm scared to come to school—I'm worried that Meredith and her friends are waiting to jump me.

I'm Meredith. Stephany thinks she can dis me and get away with it. She hates me? Okay, no problem. Wait until I catch her alone somewhere in the school. I'm going to beat that girl down for saying those things about me.

I'm Erica. You should have seen what Stephany wrote on her hand—"I hate Meredith." Where does she get off writing something like that and showing it to everyone? Then she calls Meredith fat and ugly. I went and told Meredith right away, so she would know what was up.

I'm Curtis. I heard Erica making up things about Stephany. Stephany never called Meredith fat and ugly. She doesn't even know the girl. Now Meredith is all mad and everything. But I kept out of it and didn't say anything to anyone. It's none of my business.

I'm Robert. I know people are not telling the truth. Stephany wrote "I hate Michael" on her hand, not Meredith. I'm going to tell Meredith the truth. If I don't speak up, Stephany could get hurt really badly. It's all a big misunderstanding.

Letting Go of Labels (Part 1)

Who's the Real "Problem Child"? by Marcus J. Howell

Pages 105–106 in *The Courage to Be Yourself*

overview

Story Summary

Marcus, who is in foster care, is hurt and angered when he hears a group member making hateful remarks about foster youth. But the incident also helps him to see beyond the labels people use.

Materials

- Journals

Prep Work

- Put the session's agenda on the board or flip chart (see Preview).

Objectives

Group members will:

- discuss how young people label each other

- discuss their own experiences with being labeled

- discuss how being labeled affects people

Themes

- Understanding labels and stereotypes
- Seeing beyond labels
- Respect for difference and diversity

Links to the Academic Curriculum

- Cooperative group work
- Verbal expression and point of view
- Critical thinking and analysis

THE SESSION

Preview

Preview the agenda by telling the group that today you will discuss the ways labels can hurt people, and how you can see beyond labels. To do this you will engage in the activities on this agenda:

Agenda: Letting Go of Labels

Reading: "Who's the Real 'Problem Child'?"
Gathering: Reading the Story
Activity: Letting Go of Labels
  • Summary
  • Discussion points
  • Journals
  • Large group discussion
Closing: Checking Out What We've Learned

Gathering: Reading the Story

Ask volunteers to read aloud "Who's the Real 'Problem Child'?" It is short enough that this should only take a few minutes. You may have a few volunteers read a couple paragraphs each.

Activity: Letting Go of Labels

1. Summary. Ask volunteers to summarize "Who's the Real 'Problem Child'?" in two to three sentences. You may wish to write the story summary on the board or chart paper as a reminder for the group. You may copy the summary provided on page 108 or a summary the group comes up with. (Note: Even though you have just read the story out loud, it's still a valuable exercise to have students summarize the story. Summarizing forces them to distill the main points of the story and focus on themes.)

2. Discussion points. Conduct a brief group discussion in which you introduce the concept of labels, especially the ways labels are linked to bias and stereotypes and can be used to discriminate against others. Tell the group: *In the most basic sense, a label is a word or phrase used to describe something. For example, we label parts of language as nouns, verbs, adjectives, and so on. People are also often labeled. These labels may be used to target people based on physical characteristics, ethnicity, ability level, class, gender, or other traits. Labels are a convenient way to put people in a category. It's obvious that labels such as "problem child" and "group home slut" have a negative effect on the people they label. But even labels that on the surface seem to be positive, like "class clown" or "math whiz," or ones that don't seem obviously positive or negative, like "jock" or "preppy," can have a negative effect because they reduce the person to a type.*

3. Journals. Read the first set of questions below and ask group members to respond by writing in their journals. Give them one minute to write, then read the next question aloud, again giving one minute to respond. Repeat the process for the subsequent questions. (See page 134 for a complete description of journaling.)
  Questions:

  • *Do you belong to a group of people that has been labeled by others? What labels do people use for your group?*

  • *How has being labeled affected you?*

  • *The title of this book is* **The Courage to Be Yourself.** *How does this title relate to the issue of labeling?*

- *Do you, or have you ever, labeled others? Why do (or did) you use those labels?*

- *Think of a time you heard people using labels or making hateful remarks about others. How did you react? Would you react differently now, if you had to do it over?*

4. **Large group discussion.** Ask for volunteers to discuss what they've written or talk about the prompts in a general way. Ask the group: *What can you do to reduce labeling?*

Closing: Checking Out What We've Learned

Ask for volunteers to share one thing they appreciate about your group. Model by speaking first, then invite additional responses.

Assign a story from *The Courage to Be Yourself* to be read for your group's next meeting.

Overcoming Preconceptions and Stereotypes (Part 2)

A Different Kind of Friend, by LaToya Souvenir

Pages 107–111 in *The Courage to Be Yourself*

overview

Story Summary

LaToya, an African-American, is prejudiced against Puerto Rican girls. Then she becomes good friends with Lisa, a Puerto Rican at her school, and finds out how wrong she was to believe in stereotypes.

Prep Work

- Put the session's agenda on the board or flip chart (see Preview).

Objectives

Group members will:

- review peer pressure and their reactions to it
- learn about resisting peer pressure
- learn about overcoming preconceptions and stereotypes

Themes

- Making healthy choices
- Socially responsible decision-making
- Conflict analysis

Links to the Academic Curriculum

- Point of view
- Perspective taking in literary studies
- Character analysis
- Written and verbal expression

THE SESSION

Preview

Preview the agenda by telling the group that today you will discuss the ways people can overcome their prejudices and stereotypes. To do this you will engage in the activities on this agenda:

Agenda: Overcoming Preconceptions and Stereotypes

Reading: "A Different Kind of Friend"
Gathering: Neighborhoods and Goups
Activity: Befriending Someone Different
- Summary
- Microlab
Closing: Checking Out What We've Learned

Gathering: Neighborhoods and Groups

Concentric Circles. Divide teens into two equal groups by having them count off. (If you don't have two equal groups, you can pair with one group member.) Group members should form pairs, either facing each other in two parallel rows or by forming a larger circle of group members around a smaller, inside circle. (See page 133 for a complete description of concentric circles.) Read the following questions out loud and give pairs one minute to discuss:

- *Talk about the neighborhood where you grew up as a kid. Where was it? What did it look like? What was something you liked about it?*

Then ask for volunteers to share their ideas. After a brief large group discussion, the outside circle or one of the lines should move one place to the left, so that group members are paired with a new partner. Read the next questions. Again, give the pairs one minute

to discuss and then share their answers with the whole group.

- *Name a group you belong to—such as your race, religion, a clique, gender, or another group. What is something people believe about your group that is not true?*

Repeat this process for the last questions:

- *If you could change one thing about the group you named, what would it be? Why?*

Activity: Befriending Someone Different

1. **Summary.** Ask volunteers to summarize "A Different Kind of Friend" in two to three sentences. You may wish to write the story summary on the board or chart paper as a reminder for the group. You may copy the summary provided on page 111 or a summary the group comes up with.

2. **Microlab.** Divide teens into groups of three for a microlab (if the number of group members in the group is not divisible by three, make groups of four with the extra group members). This is a timed speaking and listening activity in which group members practice good listening skills. (See page 134 for a complete description of microlabs.)

   Explain that each person will have one minute to talk to the others in the group, answering a question you will read out loud. When that person is speaking, the others are only to listen, giving the speaker their full attention, no matter how tempted they are to respond.

   Ask the first set of the following questions. Keep time for the group and let group members know when one minute has passed. At that time, the next person in the group should answer the same question. When all the people in the group have had their turns, go through the same process with each subsequent set of questions.

Questions:

- *LaToya says she was prejudiced against Lisa at first. Some of her prejudiced feelings came from her family. Does your family influence the way you view other races, cultures, or groups of people? What other things have influenced your views?*

- *We all have prejudices or the potential to believe in stereotypes. How can people overcome their prejudices or learn to see beyond their stereotypes?*

- *Was there a time when you went against what family or friends thought and befriended someone who was "different"? If so, what was the experience like? If not, describe a time you wanted to befriend someone "different" but didn't because of pressure from others.*

- *Talk about a time when you learned something about someone who belonged to a different group than you. What did you learn and how did it affect you?*

- *Describe a conflict you have witnessed at school or in your neighborhood that began or escalated because of diversity.*

Closing: Checking Out What We've Learned

Tell the group: *One interesting detail of this story is that LaToya rarely, if ever, met anyone outside her own race all the way through high school. It wasn't until she transferred out of her neighborhood school that she began to meet people from other backgrounds.*

Engage your group members in a discussion of this issue. How many of them, like LaToya, have limited exposure to people with backgrounds different from their own? Where do they get their impressions of people from other races and ethnic groups? What can they do to get more accurate impressions?

Assign a story from *The Courage to Be Yourself* to be read for your group's next meeting.

Session 24

Letting Go of Labels (Part 2)
She's Cool, She's Funny, She's Gay, by Sandra Leon

Pages 113–116 in *The Courage to Be Yourself*

overview

Story Summary

Sandra is proud of her gay sister and wishes people wouldn't stereotype her. She challenges her friends to see her sister as a person and not as someone who can be labeled.

Materials

- Forehead labels
- Masking tape

Prep Work

- Copy the Forehead Labels handout (pages 117–119) and cut out the labels. Place loops of masking tape on the back of each label. (Many of the labels included are most appropriate for older teens. For younger teens, you may want to eliminate some and add others.)

- Put the session's agenda on the board or flip chart (see Preview).

Objectives

Group members will:

- experience what it feels like to be labeled
- become more aware of their comfort zone in social situations
- relate standing up for someone to the role of an ally

Themes

- Affirmation and acceptance
- Appreciation for diversity
- Personal connections
- Building community

Links to the Academic Curriculum

- Public speaking
- Receptive language: listening
- Cooperative learning

THE SESSION

Preview

Preview the agenda by telling the group that today you will discuss ways people can overcome their prejudices and stereotypes and let go of labels. To do this you will engage in the activities on this agenda:

Agenda: Letting Go of Labels

Reading: "She's Cool, She's Funny, She's Gay"
Gathering: Group Brainstorm
Activity: The Comfort Zone
- Summary
- Large group discussion
- Forehead labels
- Large group discussion
Closing: Checking Out What We've Learned

Gathering: Group Brainstorm

Ask the group to brainstorm a list of some of the labels group members and teachers use to describe people at school. (See page 133 for a complete description of brainstorming.) Then ask whether any of these labels have positive or negative overtones. Are some labels perceived positively by some group members and negatively by others?

Activity: The Comfort Zone

1. Summary. Ask volunteers to summarize "She's Cool, She's Funny, She's Gay" in two to three sentences. You may wish to write the story summary on the board or chart paper as a reminder for the group. You may copy the summary provided on page 114 or a summary the group comes up with.

2. Large group discussion. Discuss the fact that all people have a social comfort zone. When we interact with others, we often gravitate to people we think are like us and feel uncomfortable with people we don't know or who seem different from us. For example, some straight people may have been uncomfortable around Sandra's gay sister.

Reassure group members that feeling some discomfort around people who are different from us is natural. Ask group members to make a list for themselves of three groups that they would feel most uncomfortable being with. No one else will see their lists.

Ask group members to describe—without naming the groups—why it might feel more awkward to be with some groups than with others. Group members might say, "Because I don't know what to say or do," or "I don't want to say the wrong thing and offend someone," or "I don't think they like me." Discuss the kinds of social barriers that separate people who are different from each other.

3. Forehead labels. Explain to group members that each of them will receive a forehead label that labels her or him as a member of a specific group or as an individual with a particular trait. Group members will not be able to see what's written on their labels because the labels will be stuck to their foreheads.

Place a label on the forehead of each group member. (You may want to ask a few group members to help you place the labels.) Have a limited number of different labels, with duplicates of many of them, so group members can find others who are like them. After everyone has a label, tell the group to pretend they are at a party and have 10 minutes to socialize with each other. Encourage group members to mingle with as many other group members as they can, following these rules:

- *Do not tell anyone what is written on his or her label.*

- *Respond to each person as if the label he or she is wearing is true. Engage people from groups you are comfortable with in conversations. When you encounter someone who would not be in your comfort zone, behave as you would in a real situation. If you would try to end conversations quickly, then do that. If you would try to find out more about that person or group, then do that. Try to react in a genuine way.*

When 10 minutes are up say, "Freeze." Ask group members to think about how people reacted to them. Did they feel like they got friendly, hostile, or confused responses from their peers? Ask all group members who think they had a positive label to stand on one side of the room. Ask all group members who think they had a negative label to stand on the other side of the room. Ask group members who felt they received both positive and negative responses to their label to stand in the middle. (Most of the labels don't have obviously positive or negative connotations, but group members will likely perceive positive or negative reactions.)

4. **Large group discussion.** Ask for volunteers from all three groups to explain what

people said or did that made them feel their label was positive, negative, or a little of both. What comments or questions gave group members clues about their label? It's especially important to discuss how group members reacted physically to others (facial expressions and physical gestures). Tell group members that a great deal of communication is nonverbal. People often give away what they're thinking about without saying a word.

Ask if any group members think they know what their label says. Ask for volunteers to guess, then take off the label and read it. Then let the rest of the group take off their labels and read them.

Closing: Checking Out What We've Learned

Ask the group:

- *What labels do you think hurt people the most or make people the angriest? Why?*

- *What can you do personally, or through organizations at school, to help group members stretch beyond their personal social comfort zones and get to know people who are different from them?*

To help your group answer this last question, ask them to consider:

- *Where and with whom do you sit in class?*

- *Who gets invited to participate in special projects at school?*

- *Are there unspoken rules about who does what at school?*

- *Are there many opportunities to talk with students who are different from you?*

Assign a story from *The Courage to Be Yourself* to be read for your group's next meeting.

ForeHEAD LABELS

I'm a recent immigrant and I don't speak English well.	I'm a bully.
I get bullied a lot.	I have a short temper.
I'm shy.	I use a wheelchair.
I don't believe in God.	I'm very religious.

Continued ➡

My family is very wealthy.	My family is poor.
The kids I hang out with like making fun of others.	I'm single and like not having a boyfriend or girlfriend.
I'm African American and hang out with only African Americans.	I like doing well in school.
I don't always wear the latest fashions.	My friends smoke pot but I refuse.

Continued →

I'm very overweight.	My friends are into hip hop but I prefer listening to musicals.
I live in a housing project.	I'm in foster care.
I hang out with kids from lots of different groups.	I sit with the unpopular kids in the school cafeteria.
I smile a lot and am very friendly.	Some of my friends are gang members.

Session 25

Introduction to Mediation

Back Off: Peer Mediation Can Help, by Zainab Muhammad

Pages 117–119 in *The Courage to Be Yourself*

overview

Story Summary

When Zainab gets into a fight with another girl at school, she discovers the power of peer mediation in solving conflicts.

Materials

- Board or flip chart paper
- 3" x 5" index cards
- Handout: The Mediation Process

Prep Work

- Write the definitions of *mediation*, *arbitration*, and *negotiation* (provided in Activity 1) on the board or flip chart paper for discussion.
- Put the session's agenda on the board or flip chart paper (see Preview).
- Make a copy of the Mediation Process handout (pages 123–124) for everyone in the group.

Objectives

Students will:

- understand the difference between the definitions of *mediation*, *arbitration*, and *negotiation*
- practice identifying what mediation is and is not
- observe and analyze the mediation process

Themes

- Managing and resolving conflict
- Caring and effective communication
- Cooperation and collaborative problem-solving
- Shared decision-making
- Point of view and perspective taking

Links to the Academic Curriculum

- Student government and leadership
- Theater and drama
- Character analysis
- Character education

THE SESSION

Preview

Preview the agenda by telling the class that today you will discuss how a process called mediation can help solve conflicts. To do this you will engage in the activities on this agenda:

Agenda: Introduction to Mediation

Reading: "Back Off: Peer Mediation Can Help"
Gathering: Resolving Conflict
Activity 1: Defining Mediation, Arbitration, and Negotiation
- Summary
- Definitions
Activity 2: Mediation Discussion and Demonstration
- Popcorn-style sharing
- Handout
- Role-plays
- Large group discussion
Closing: Checking Out What We've Learned

Gathering: Resolving Conflict

Conduct a group discussion of the following questions: *Besides fighting or arguing, what can you do to resolve conflict? What are some example situations?*

Activity 1: Defining Mediation, Arbitration, and Negotiation

1. Summary. Ask volunteers to summarize "Back Off: Peer Mediation Can Help" in two to three sentences. You may wish to write the story summary on the board or chart paper as a reminder for the class. You may copy the summary provided on page 120 or a summary that the group comes up with.

2. Definitions. Read through the following definitions, which you've written on the board or flip chart paper.

Mediation: Process in which two disputants (people who are having a conflict) allow a neutral third person, the mediator, to help develop a solution to their conflict. A mediator helps the disputants reach a solution they both can accept, but does not take sides or impose a solution.

Arbitration: Process in which a neutral third party imposes a binding decision on two disputants. Usually used when disputants cannot reach an agreement themselves. Instead, they agree to allow an arbitrator to impose a binding agreement on them.

Negotiation: Process in which two disputing parties, sometimes with a third party, work out a compromise or mutually agreeable solution. If it doesn't work, it usually results in arbitration.

Conduct a group discussion about the definitions by asking if there are any questions and having group members consider what might be the strengths and weaknesses of each method.

Activity 2: Mediation Discussion and Demonstration

1. Popcorn-style sharing. Form a large circle with the group and explain how popcorn-style sharing works: everyone may share their thoughts at any time, and there is no pressure to participate. (See page 135 for a complete description of popcorn-style sharing.) Ask students if they have seen or participated in a resolution process as described in Zainab's story, where someone helped others settle a conflict, or if they have been in an argument where someone tried to help them.

2. **Handout.** Distribute the Mediation Process handout and read through the steps with your group. Answer any questions that come up as you go along.

   When you're done going through the handout, write the word "mediator" on the board. Ask students to suggest what qualities one should possess in order to be a good mediator (for example, listens well, is fair, is creative).

3. **Role-plays.** Ask two students to help you role-play the conflict between Zainab and Vicki from the story (or use one you have invented based on common conflicts among your group members) to demonstrate the process. You, the leader, will play the role of the mediator. (See page 135 for a complete description of role-plays.)

   Scenario (using the conflict from the story): A boy insults Zainab in class and she insults him back. Vicki butts in and gets in a shouting match with Zainab. Zainab and Vicki are sent to peer mediation.

   In the role-play, students may add dialogue between Zainab and Vicki that was not included in the story, imagining what they might have felt and what they might have said to one another both during the fight and during mediation. Act out all the steps of mediation, through the successful resolution of the conflict. Use the Mediation Process handout as a guide. Instruct the actors to go along with your mediation efforts rather than resist them.

4. **Large group discussion.** After the demonstration, ask the class:

   - *What did each person want? What feelings did each person bring to the mediation?*
   - *How did the solution meet important needs of both parties?*
   - *What questions helped the disputants reach a good solution?*

Closing: Checking Out What We've Learned

On 3" x 5" index cards, ask students to list the two or three things they think are most important for the mediator to say or do in the mediation process. Collect the cards and read them out loud.

Assign a story from *The Courage to Be Yourself* to be read for your group's next meeting.

THE MEDIATION PROCESS

1. Setting the Stage

▶ Ask those involved in the conflict if they would like your help solving the problem. Get agreement on this.

▶ Find a quiet place to do the mediation.

▶ Explain that you will help them come up with their own solution. You won't take sides or give advice or tell them how to solve the problem.

▶ Ask the disputants to agree that they will:

  ■ try to solve the problem

  ■ not engage in name-calling or personal attacks

  ■ not interrupt when the other person is speaking

  ■ be as honest as they can

  ■ keep everything that is said during the mediation confidential

2. Getting the Stories Out

▶ Ask disputant 1, "What happened?" After she or he has finished, restate what was said and ask clarifying questions, such as "How did you feel?"

▶ Ask disputant 2, "What happened?" After she or he has finished, restate what was said and ask clarifying questions, such as "How did you feel?"

▶ Ask each disputant to restate how the other person feels and why.

▶ Ask each disputant what she or he needs in order to feel like the conflict is resolved.

▶ Ask, "Is there anything else?" Then summarize the whole problem, including key facts and feelings that have been shared by both disputants. Identify common interests and concerns and anything that both disputants feel is important to remember as they work out a solution.

Continued ➡

3. Brainstorming Solutions

▶ Ask disputant 1, "What can you do here and now to help solve the problem?" Encourage him or her to be specific. Restate what disputant 1 says.

▶ Ask disputant 2, "What can you do here and now to help solve the problem?" Encourage him or her to be specific. Restate what disputant 2 says.

▶ If they get stuck, ask, "What would you tell someone with a similar problem to do? How would this solution work? Can you think of something else you could do? Can you say more about your idea?"

4. Resolution

▶ Help the disputants reach a solution that works for both of them. Help them make the solution specific: who does what, when, where, and how?

▶ Restate the solution and all of its parts to the disputants.

▶ Ask each person individually if he or she agrees to the solution they have chosen.

▶ Ask both disputants, "What can you each do differently if this happens again?" Restate their ideas.

▶ Congratulate them on a successful mediation.

How Can People Make a Difference?

My School Is Like a Family, by T. Shawn Welcome

Pages 121–124 in *The Courage to Be Yourself*

Note: This is a two-part session, with each part conducted at least one week apart so that students can plan, develop, and make presentations to the class. You may want to introduce the first activity several weeks in advance of the second, to give group members adequate time to plan and carry out their presentations. We also recommend doing this session last.

overview

Story Summary

After transferring from a large, impersonal high school, T. Shawn finds a family among the teachers and students at his small, alternative school.

Materials

- Group Assessment Questionnaire handout

Prep Work

- Establish a feasible timeline for the project. You may want to put it on a handout or simply write it on the board or flip chart paper. If you wish, include project guidelines on the handout (see Activity 1).

- If this will be your group's final session, make a copy of the Group Assessment Questionnaire handout (pages 130–132) for everyone in the group.

- Put the session's agenda on the board or flip chart (see Preview).

Objectives

Group members will:

- brainstorm a list of people in their school or community who are making a positive difference

- interview one person who is making a difference in the school or community

- write a report about the interview

- present the results of the interview to the group

Themes

- Social responsibility
- Personal connections

Links to the Academic Curriculum

- Verbal and written expression
- Public speaking
- Career and job skills
- Service learning

THE SESSION

Preview

Preview the agenda by telling the class that today you will discuss how people can make a difference in their schools and communities. To do this you will engage in the activities on this agenda:

Agenda: How Can People Make a Difference?

Reading: "My School Is Like a Family"
Gathering: Help Go-Round
Activity 1: The Making a Difference Project
  • Summary
  • Introduction
  • Preparation
  • Guidelines
  • Due dates
Activity 2: The Making a Difference Project Presentations
  • Presentations
  • Posters and charts
Closing: Checking Out What We've Learned

Gathering: Help Go-Round

In a go-round, ask group members to describe a time when they helped out a friend or relative who needed assistance. Invite them to share how they felt after this experience. (See page 133 for a complete description of go-rounds.)

Activity 1: The Making a Difference Project

1. Summary. Ask volunteers to summarize "My School Is Like a Family" in two to three sentences. You may wish to write the story summary on the board or chart paper as

a reminder for the class. You may copy the summary provided on page 125 or a summary that the group comes up with.

2. Introduction. Explain to the group that they will interview an adult or teen whose efforts have made a positive difference in her or his school or community. They will document their experience in a written narrative and share it in a presentation to the class. Present your timeline for the project as a handout or on the board for the group to copy down. Include dates for finalizing choices of subjects, completing the interviews, finishing the written report, and presenting projects to the group. You may allow group members to work individually or in pairs.

3. Preparation. Present the following list of suggestions to help spark some ideas, then ask group members to brainstorm their own lists of specific people to interview.

  • *An adult whose job it is to make and/or keep the peace—for example, a principal, dean, security guard, or police officer.*

  • *An adult who helps make life better for teens in difficult situations—for example, a guidance counselor, social worker, school psychologist, school nurse, substance abuse counselor, diversity or human relations coordinator, mentor, or tutor.*

  • *An adult who is involved in extracurricular programs at the school or in the community—for example, a sports coach, debate coach, student paper advisor, academic club advisor, or community/youth theater director.*

- *A favorite teacher or community leader, or a teacher or leader who has had an impact on a student's life.*

- *A student who has made a contribution to the school or community—for example, through academic achievement, sports, creative ability, student government, peer relations, volunteering, extracurricular activities, or school clubs.*

Next, brainstorm a list of questions with the group that group members will use to structure their interviews. You may use the following samples to get started.

Sample interview questions for adults:

- How did you decide to do this kind of work?

- What kind of training and education is required for this work?

- What are the best and worst parts of the job?

- What is one story you could tell that would help others understand the importance of your work?

- How do you feel you help others the most?

Sample interview questions for teens:

- Why did you decide to get involved in this activity (program, team, and so on)?

- How is this school or community important to you?

- How do you feel you have contributed to making the school or community a better place?

- What advice would you give other young people about getting involved and contributing to their school or community?

4. **Guidelines.** You may establish project guidelines ahead of time and include them on your timeline handout, or you may create guidelines with your group during the session. Make sure you create guidelines that cover:

- criteria for the written narratives, such as length and point of view. Point of view options might include a first-person account of the writer's experience or a more formal third-person portrait of the subject.

- criteria for presentations, including time limit and format. Format options might include whether they should use visual aids (photographs, artwork, videos, and so on) or computer presentation software, or whether they can invite the subject to speak with the group.

- if they will give presentations to the whole group or within smaller groups. The schedule and time limit you establish should reflect this (that is, if every student is to give a presentation to the whole group, a short time limit and two days for presentations may be necessary).

5. **Due dates.** After this set-up meeting, have group members report to you regarding due dates on the timeline. They should inform you of their choice for a profile subject, complete their interviews, and turn in their essays all by the due dates on the timeline. They should have at least one week before essays and presentations are due.

Activity 2: The Making A Difference Project Presentations

1. **Presentations.** Continue the session at least a week later, when group members will make their presentations. If they will give presentations within smaller groups,

break them into groups of three or four. Have each group member present his or her project within his or her group or to the class as a whole.

2. **Posters and charts.** When all the presentations are finished, divide the teens into groups of three or four if they're not already in them. Have each group make a poster, chart, or web titled You Can Make a Difference. The poster, chart, or web should reflect what they shared today and focus on the ways they can make a difference. Allow 10 to 15 minutes for groups to do the project.

Closing: Checking Out What We've Learned

Have each group present its poster, chart, or web to the larger group. Ask each group to explain how they decided what to put on their poster, chart, or web.

Pass out copies of the Group Assessment Questionnaire. Ask group members to complete it in class if time allows or as homework if you'll be meeting again.

Sessions Group Assessment

Whether you used only a few sessions from this guide or conducted an extensive series of sessions with your group, it's important to get feedback from the group members on their experiences in the sessions in order to help you improve or change them when you lead them in the future. Because the content is so personal and deeply connected to group members' experiences, feedback will help you determine what works best and resonates most with young people, so you can teach the subject in the most effective way possible. Use the following questionnaire to get that feedback.

Note: To encourage group members to spend more time on each question and produce more thoughtful responses, you may choose to have them respond to only five questions instead of all 10. You may highlight the ones you want them to answer or you may invite them to select the five they want to answer. Also, consider that the number of sessions you conducted may influence which questions will be the most appropriate.

Group Assessment Questionnaire

1. What are three things you want to remember most from these sessions?

   _____

   _____

   _____

2. What are two of the most important things you've learned from these sessions?

   _____

   _____

   _____

3. What's a skill you've learned and used that has changed your relationship with someone?

   _____

   _____

   _____

4. Has learning more about cultural diversity changed your ideas and feelings about people who belong to different cultural groups from you? How?

   _____

   _____

   _____

5. Have these sessions changed your ideas and feelings about prejudice and discrimination? How?

   _____

   _____

   _____

Continued ➡

6. Has the meaning of any of these words changed for you during this course? How?

Respect _____

_____

Community _____

_____

Conflict _____

_____

Listening _____

_____

Violence _____

_____

Peacemaking _____

_____

Nonviolence _____

_____

Assertiveness _____

_____

7. What aspect, issue, or activity in the sessions was most challenging? Was anything in the sessions difficult for you to do or hard to confront?

_____

_____

Continued ➡

8. What two or three issues and/or activities do you wish all students in your school or community could experience? Why would you recommend these issues or activities?

_____

_____

_____

_____

_____

9. What might you be more aware of or do differently because you participated in these sessions?

_____

_____

_____

_____

_____

10. Are there any changes you would make in the sessions to make them more effective?

_____

_____

_____

_____

_____

Teaching and Learning Strategies

Here are descriptions of the teaching and learning strategies used in this leader's guide. Feel free to adapt your own strategies to the sessions.

Brainstorming

A process for generating as many ideas as possible. The leader proposes a topic or question and lists group members' responses on the board or on chart paper. Here are a few helpful brainstorming guidelines to share with your group:

- All ideas are accepted; every idea will be written down.

- No one makes a comment, either positive or negative, on any of the ideas presented.

- Push for quantity. Say anything that comes to mind, even if it sounds silly.

- Think about what others have suggested and use those ideas to get your brain moving along new lines.

Concentric Circles

This activity gives group members a chance to share with a variety of partners. Divide the teens into two equal groups. (If you don't have two equal groups, you can join one.) One group forms a circle facing outward. The other group forms a second circle around that one, facing inward. Each person in the inner circle faces a partner in the outer circle. (If you don't have enough space to make circles, parallel rows

will suffice.) Tell the group that they will each have about 45 seconds to share with their partners and that all pairs will speak simultaneously (pair members take turns). Identify whether the inside partners or the outside partners will speak first. Pose a question to the group and begin timing. When time is up, the other partners respond to the question. When both partners have answered the question, ask one of the circles to move one, two, or three spaces to the right. Then pose another question and repeat the process. To ensure group members interact with a range of partners, the circle should rotate for each question. Concentric circles is less intimate than other group sharing activities, such as microlabs and pair shares, and is more appropriate for less sensitive or difficult topics. For example, in Session 3: What Is Harassment?, we use concentric circles with a question that focuses on the story rather than on the group members themselves. It's also good for situations when you want teens to get multiple responses and be more active. It helps build class unity and group participation.

Go-Rounds

Gives every member of the group a chance to respond to a statement or question. This activity is especially useful for sharing feelings and experiences. In go-rounds, the group is seated in a circle (if possible). Circles greatly facilitate open communication by putting everyone on an equal footing, especially when the leader joins the group. In addition, everyone in the group can look directly at the person who is speaking. This encourages everyone to pay attention to one another and fosters a sense of community.

Introduce the topic of the go-round in the form of a statement or question. The topic can be general so that most group members will be able to comment (for example, "What was something you enjoyed about our last session?"), or it can be something specifically related to the content of a session. Group members take turns responding, going around the circle. People always have the right to pass when it's their turn to speak, though even those who find it difficult to speak in groups often will speak during a go-round. After everyone has responded, you can go back to those who passed to see if they now want to contribute.

Journal Writing

Teens can explore conflict through various writing activities. Several sessions ask group members to respond to questions in journals. You may want to distribute journals to the group before the first session and ask them to record their reactions to the sessions as you progress. Journal prompts urge group members to review conflicts they have experienced, examine feelings and opinions they hold, and brainstorm or discuss ideas. Journal entries do not have to be long—it is the ability to connect with feelings and experiences that counts, not the length of the entry. Assure the group their journal writing will not be graded or collected, and no one will be required to share what they have written.

In some sessions we provide a series of journal prompts. In these sessions, you will read aloud a statement or question and ask the students to write their responses in their journals. Offer the group only a *short* time to

write on each question (one minute is fine; three minutes is the maximum). Tell them they must keep writing without stopping (writing nonstop frees up emotions and ideas). If they say they don't have anything to write, tell them they can keep writing "I have nothing to say" until something comes to them. When time is up, read the next prompt, again allowing a short period of time for responding.

In our experiences with teens we've found that a few minutes of freewriting deepens their reflections and often opens up topics for discussion that would not otherwise be raised by discussion alone.

Microlabs

Enables participants to examine their experiences in the intimacy of a small group. It is designed to maximize personal sharing and active listening. In groups of three or four, group members take turns responding to questions. Each person has an equal period of time to respond. When one person is speaking, others give the speaker their full attention and do not interrupt or ask questions. Speakers should use I-Messages when discussing what they said, thought, and felt. When introducing microlabs, stress the importance of confidentiality. What is shared in a microlab should not be repeated outside the group.

Opinion Continuums

This technique allows group members to express their own attitudes and opinions and, most importantly, to realize that it is okay to hold a different opinion from others in the class. To begin activities using this technique, draw a line on the board or on the floor with "Strongly Agree" at one end, "Strongly Disagree" at the other, and "Unsure" in the middle. You then read a statement and group members position themselves along the line to indicate their opinions. Alternatively, you can use a person or object in the room as a symbol and ask group members to position themselves according to how they feel about the thing being symbolized. For example, in Session 9: Responding to Conflict—What Do We Do? (Part 1), you conduct a conflict opinion continuum. In this activity, the leader represents conflict and group members stand either close to or far from you depending on how comfortable they are dealing with conflict. After group members have positioned themselves in the opinion continuum, you can invite them to explain their positions.

Pair Shares

This technique involves multiple, simultaneous conversations. Students share responses to a question in one of two ways: One student focuses on practicing listening skills while the other partner speaks, then partners switch roles; students engage in a dialogue with each other and agree on a response to share with the larger group. Like microlabs, pair shares are more intimate than large group–centered activities, such as concentric circles or popcorn-style sharing. When you want group members to come up with deeper, more thoughtful responses, a pair share is a good option.

Popcorn-Style Sharing

This method promotes free expression of ideas in a nonjudgmental atmosphere. A set amount of time (usually about four minutes) is allotted for the whole group to share ideas on a topic—it works best when group members sit in a circle. You may pose the topic, or invite teens to bring up a theme from the assigned reading. Popcorn-style sharing means that

rather than going around the circle one by one, students voice their opinions in a random order. There is no pressure to speak up.

Role-Plays

A fun opportunity to assume a different perspective and perform in small groups. Give students scenarios (which are provided in the sessions) and stage names, or let them pick their own names (names of students currently in the group are off limits). List each character's role on the board, as a prompt. Review the roles with students before starting, then have them act out the scenario. Remind the actors to stay in character for the duration of the role-play. Here are some basic guidelines:

- Set a time limit of no longer than five minutes per role-play.
- Allow no physical contact between participants and no cursing or other inappropriate language.
- Have the other group members observe the role-play closely and be prepared to share their reactions when it's over.

Rotation Stations

This technique allows teens to brainstorm responses to a series of questions in a small group. Write questions or problems on large sheets of newsprint or chart paper and post the questions in different areas around the room. Divide teens into groups of three or four and ask each smaller group to stand at one of the stations. Give them two minutes to brainstorm two or three responses to the question or problem. Have them write their responses on the newsprint or chart paper, then ask each group to move to the next station and give their responses to another question.

Webbing or Concept Maps

Choose a key word or concept from the session story and write it in the center of the board or flip chart. Ask the group to suggest words and ideas they associate with that word or concept. Add the new words and ideas to the board with a line stemming out from the word in the center. To visually connect various aspects of the key concept and the following associations, you can cluster related ideas together. For example, in Session 3: What Is Harassment?, the group creates a harassment web, recording whatever thoughts, words, feelings, and behaviors come to mind when they hear the word *harassment*.

Resources

American Association of University Women (AAUW)
1111 Sixteenth Street NW
Washington, DC 20036
1-800-326-AAUW (1-800-326-2289)
www.aauw.org

AAUW's mission is to promote equal access and equity in the academic lives of girls and young women. Among its publications is "Hostile Hallways: Bullying, Teasing, and Harassment in School," a report on sexual harassment in schools. AAUW also offers research focused on young women's attitudes toward and responses to peer pressure, sexuality, media, and school.

Anti-Defamation League (ADL)
823 UN Plaza
New York, NY 10017
212-490-2525
www.adl.org

A nonprofit organization dedicated to the promotion of civil rights and combating anti-Semitism and all forms of racism and bigotry. Offering training in the *A World of Difference Institute* program, the institute's goals include helping participants recognize the affect of bias, racism, and anti-Semitism on individuals and society. ADL curriculum is used by schools, law enforcement agencies, and community agencies to dismantle racism and bigotry and promote respect for all people.

Bridges to Safety: Help Teens Teach Conflict Resolution and Character Skills to Children by Maureen Campbell and Sharon Yoerg (San Mateo, CA: Six Seconds, 2004).

A book and CD-ROM resource set for youth leaders and educators to train teens in peaceful problem solving and leadership skills.

Bullying.org
www.bullying.org

A comprehensive resource that provides information on articles, books, films, legislation, policies, research, and related resources for use in schools and community-based settings.

Character Education Partnership (CEP)
1025 Connecticut Avenue NW, Suite 1011
Washington, DC 20036
1-800-988-8081
www.character.org

CEP provides print and Web-based resources related to character education. They offer several links to research-based reports and curricula that help schools infuse character education into the standard curriculum.

Conflict Resolution in the Schools: A Manual for Educators by Kathryn Girard and Susan J. Koch (New York: Jossey-Bass, 1996).

This guide for educators includes material developed by the National Institute for Dispute Resolution and the National Association for Mediation in Education. Discussion topics and training tools focus on conflict management and mediation in schools.

"Early Warning, Timely Response: A Guide to Safe Schools" by K. Dwyer, D. Osher, and C. Warger (Washington, DC: U.S. Department of Education Office of Special Education and Rehabilitative Services, 1998).

Based on the work of an independent panel of education, law enforcement, and mental health experts, this guide helps identify and promote the qualities of safe and responsive schools. Created in response to increases in school violence, including harassment and bullying. Available from the U.S. Department of Education (www.ed.gov/about/offices/list/osers/osep/gtss.html). 1-877-4EDPUBS (1-877-433-7827).

Gay, Lesbian and Straight Education Network (GLSEN)
90 Broad Street, Second Floor
New York, NY 10004
212-727-0135
www.glsen.org

The largest national educational network of parents, students, and educators working to make schools safe and supportive environments for gay, lesbian, bisexual, and trans-gendered youth. Believing that education is the key to eliminating anti-gay prejudice and hate-motivated violence, the network provides information on civil rights, school safety, and curriculum in order to help make schools safe and supportive for all students.

The Harvard Education Letter
www.edletter.org
1-800-513-0763

This award-winning newsletter reports, interprets, and critiques new research and innovative practice in preK–12 education. Its mission is to publish concise, accurate, thought-provoking articles that educators and parents can understand and use. It reports on the work of teachers and research-ers throughout the world, approaching timely issues such as violence and conflict resolution from multiple perspectives.

Human Rights Campaign (HRC)
1640 Rhode Island Avenue NW
Washington, DC 20036
202-628-4160
www.hrc.org

An organization that works to advance equal-ity based on sexual orientation and gender expression and identity, to ensure that gay, lesbian, bisexual, and transgender Americans can be open, honest, and safe at home, at work, and in the community. HRC's National Coming Out Project features resources for youth and parents that promote honesty and authentic dialogue among friends, family, par-ents, and coworkers of older gay teens. Among the resources offered is *Coming Out as a Straight Ally* (www.tinyurl.com/4lhb2).

The Kids' Guide to Working Out Conflicts and corresponding **Leader's Guide** by Naomi Drew (Minneapolis: Free Spirit Publishing, 2004).

Conflict-resolution strategies, anger manage-ment practices, and plans for coping with bul-lying and other social problems for kids 10–14.

**U.S. Department of Education
Office of Safe and Drug Free Schools**
Washington, DC 20202
1-800-USA-LEARN (1-800-872-5327)
www.ed.gov/offices/OESE/SDFS/index.html

Works to reduce violence and drug, alcohol, and tobacco use in schools through education and advocacy. Its Web site offers free resources and publications for students, parents, teachers, and administrators.

Parents, Families and Friends of Lesbians and Gays (PFLAG)
1726 M Street NW, Suite 400
Washington, DC 20036
202-467-8180
www.pflag.org

Promotes the health and well-being of gay, lesbian, bisexual, and transgendered individuals and their families and friends by providing resources and support, education, and advocacy. PFLAG has support services available in most communities in the United States.

School Mediation Associates (SMA)
134 W. Standish Road
Watertown, MA 02472
1-800-833-3318
www.schoolmediation.com

The mission of School Mediation Associates is to transform schools into safer, more caring, and more effective institutions. SMA offers mediation, facilitation, and training services for educators, students, and parents.

The Southern Poverty Law Center (SPLC)
400 Washington Avenue
Montgomery, AL 36104
334-956-8200
www.splcenter.org

A nonprofit organization and watchdog group that works to end hate, racism, and discrimination and to promote tolerance and acceptance of all people through education and litigation. SPLC provides resources for parents, administrators, teachers, and students, and provides online professional development and classroom-based resources for educators of K–12 students through its education program, Teaching Tolerance (www.tolerance.org/teach). With news links, self-assessments, curricula, videos, and an online forum for connecting with other teachers, parents, and students, this site is dedicated to reducing hate, bias, and all forms of discrimination in schools.

Teaching Peace
P.O. Box 412
Hygiene, CO 80533
303-772-9070
www.teachingpeace.org

This nonprofit agency is dedicated to fostering attitudes, skills, and opportunities for living peacefully. It offers seminars, workshop and curriculum materials, teaching tips, and other resource materials for educators and parents on conflict prevention and resolution.

What Do You Stand For? For Teens: A Guide to Building Character by Barbara A. Lewis (Minneapolis: Free Spirit Publishing, 2005).

Quotations, dilemmas, activities, and true stories inspire teens to build strong, positive character traits including honesty, kindness, empathy, integrity, tolerance, patience, respect, and more. Includes reproducibles.

Writing as a Way of Healing: How Telling Our Stories Transforms Our Lives by Louise DeSalvo (San Francisco: HarperCollins, 1999).

This book includes suggestions and encouragement for using creative writing to work through emotional pain or trauma.

Resources from Educators for Social Responsibility

For a complete list of ESR resources visit www.esrnational.org.

Countering Bullying and Harassment: A Facilitator's Guide to an Effective Peer Education Program in Middle and High Schools by Heather Coulehan and Sherrie Gammage (Cambridge, MA: Educators for Social Responsibility, 2006).

School can be a hostile and unfriendly environment characterized by fear, isolation, and unhappiness for students who are bullied or harassed by their peers. This book presents a comprehensive peer education approach to tackling this problem. It includes the training agenda and lessons on topics such as peer pressure, healthy friendships, and dealing with rumors.

Conflict Resolution in the High School by Carol Miller Lieber (Cambridge, MA: Educators for Social Responsibility, 1998).

This comprehensive, sequenced curriculum helps secondary educators address conflict resolution and problem solving; build community and create a Peaceable Classroom; strengthen intergroup relations; and aid social and emotional development. It includes sections on implementation, assessment, and infusion of conflict resolution throughout a standard curriculum.

Conflict Resolution in the Middle School by William J. Kreidler (Cambridge, MA: Educators for Social Responsibility, 1997).

This highly acclaimed guide features 28 skill-building sections to help students address the conflicts that come with adolescence. It includes seven implementation models; sections on creating a classroom for teaching conflict resolution, developing staff and parent support, and assessing student learning; an infusion section that includes math and science; and a section on adolescent development exploring gender and race.

Partners in Learning by Carol Miller Lieber (Cambridge, MA: Educators for Social Responsibility, 2002).

A practical, hands-on guide organized around 10 core practices that will enable students and teachers to work together toward common learning goals. Each practice includes classroom-tested tools, strategies, and routines that make a positive difference in students' motivation to learn and succeed. This guide also includes a chapter on classroom management and discipline, a guide for setting up the classroom to support these practices, and a detailed plan for integrating community building, student orientation, and course content into the first month of school. With hundreds of activities and tips, this guide is an essential for every high school classroom teacher.

The Advisory Guide by Rachel A. Poliner and Carol Miller Lieber (Cambridge, MA: Educators for Social Responsibility, 2004).

School leaders agree that advisory is a core structure for personalizing schooling for adolescents. The challenge is crafting the best program for your students and faculty. This comprehensive guide presents snapshots of various advisory models and helps planning teams think through nine major issues that should be addressed in order for the program and faculty advisors to get off to a good start. The implementation chapters offer facilitation tips, suggestions for using 15 different formats, and over 130 sample activities organized around 10 advisory themes, including student orientation, community building, tools for school and learning, goal setting and assessment, life skills, and career exploration. Perfect for large and small schools, independent and public, *The Advisory Guide* is a must-have resource for anyone involved in advisory from study groups and committees thinking through implementation to the advisors in the classroom.

Resources from Youth Communication

For a complete list of Youth Communication resources visit www.youthcomm.org.

The Courage to Be Yourself edited by Al Desetta, with Educators for Social Responsibility (Minneapolis: Free Spirit Publishing, 2005).

In 26 first-person stories, real teens write about their experiences of peer conflict with searing honesty. They will inspire young readers to reflect on their own lives, work through their problems, and learn who they really are.

Fighting the Monster: Teens Write About Confronting Emotional Challenges and Getting Help edited by Al Desetta (New York: Youth Communication, 2004).

This book contains 39 true stories by teens about getting help for depression, cutting, sexual abuse, domestic violence, substance abuse, eating disorders, bereavement, promiscuity, uncontrolled anger, and many other topics. Teens describe what worked for them, including self-help, therapy, and medication.

The Heart Knows Something Different: Teenage Voices from the Foster Care System edited by Al Desetta (New York: Persea Books, 1996).

Fifty-one powerful stories by foster youth that explore family, living in the system, personal reflection, and looking to the future.

Out With It: Gay and Straight Teens Write About Homosexuality edited by Philip Kay, Andrea Estepa, and Al Desetta (New York: Youth Communication, 1996).

Sensitive issues of teen sexuality, coming out, homophobia, and relationships with family and friends are explored in articles authored by teens. Includes a 25-page "Resources for Teachers" section.

Starting With I: Personal Essays by Teenagers edited by Andrea Estepa and Philip Kay (New York: Persea Books, 1997).

"Who am I and who do I want to become?" Thirty-five stories examine this question through the lenses of race, ethnicity, gender, sexuality, family, and more. Free *Teacher's Guide* is also available.

The Struggle to Be Strong: True Stories by Teens About Overcoming Tough Times edited by Al Desetta and Sybil Wolin (Minneapolis: Free Spirit Publishing, 2000).

In 30 first-person stories, teens tell how they faced and overcame major life obstacles. Readers learn about seven resiliencies— insight, independence, relationships, initiative, creativity, humor, and morality—that everyone needs to triumph over adversity.

A Leader's Guide to The Struggle to Be Strong by Al Desetta and Sybil Wolin (Minneapolis: Free Spirit Publishing, 2000).

Thirty sessions link the stories from *The Struggle to Be Strong* with the seven resiliencies. Activities, exercises, and discussions help teens go deeper into the stories, relate them to their own lives, and build resiliency skills. Includes reproducible handouts.

Things Get Hectic: Teens Write About the Violence That Surrounds Them edited by Philip Kay, Andrea Estepa, and Al Desetta (New York: Touchstone, 1998).

Violence is commonplace in many teens' lives, whether from bullying, gangs, dating, or family relationships. Hear the experiences of victims, perpetrators, and witnesses through more than 50 real-world stories.

New Youth Connections, a general-interest teen magazine.

Represent: The Voice of Youth in Care, a magazine written by and for young people in foster care.

In addition, Youth Communication publishes dozens of booklets on a wide range of youth issues.

About Educators for Social Responsibility

ESR is a national nonprofit organization that was founded in 1982. Its mission is to make teaching social responsibility a core practice in education so that young people develop the convictions and skills to shape a safe, sustainable, democratic, and just world.

The organization is a national leader in educational reform. Its work spans the fields of social and emotional learning, character education, conflict resolution, diversity education, civic engagement, prevention programming, youth development, and secondary school improvement. ESR offers comprehensive programs, staff development, consultation, and resources for adults who teach children and young people in preschool through high school, in settings including K–12 schools, early childhood centers, and after-school programs.

ESR works in three broad areas:

- Student skill development: ESR works with teachers to help students develop social skills, emotional competencies, and qualities of character that increase interpersonal effectiveness, and reduce intolerance and aggressive, anti-social behavior.

- School and classroom climate: ESR helps schools create safe, caring, respectful, and disciplined learning environments that promote healthy development and academic success for all students.

- Response to social crises and world events: ESR helps educators respond effectively to local, national, and international crises related to interpersonal and systemic violence, intolerance, and global conflicts and war.

ESR's Countering Bullying and Harassment Program

ESR helps middle and high schools address the critical problems of bullying and harassment, and create school environments that are safer, more respectful, and more conducive to learning for all students. The Countering Harassment and Bullying Program will lead to greater recognition by staff and students of bullying and harassment; increased empathy for those targeted by other students; greater willingness among students to take a stand against bullying and harassment directed toward themselves and others; increased skillfulness among staff to intervene when necessary; a decrease in incidents of bullying and harassment; and an increase in feelings of safety and security among students.

When you work with ESR, you'll get innovative materials and experienced consultants who guide you through the stages of setting up a successful peer education program. ESR will help you assess the climate at your school, including the specific dynamics related to bullying and harassment, and think about how other school initiatives that are already underway can complement your program. ESR trains a carefully selected cross-section of students along with a program coordinator and small group of other adults who will help support the program. They will explore the nature of safe and healthy friendships and learn ways to deal effectively with peer pressure and stop rumors. The group will learn what constitutes bullying and harassment. They will examine its sources and dynamics, including the different types of bullying and harassment that people face, from gender and sexual orientation, or race and ethnicity, to size and looks. They'll gain confidence and skills for becoming an ally who interrupts bullying and harassment rather than a bystander or an instigator.

After two days of training for the staff and two days of training for the adults and students together, the students will be prepared to make a series of presentations to their peers throughout the school. Presentations can take place through a variety of forums including health and PE classes, social studies and language arts courses, and advisory groups. In addition, ESR will work with the entire staff to consider other ways that adults can help improve the climate in the school and build a culture of respect as well as make presentations for parents about what they can do to respond to bullying and harassment and to inform them about the peer education program.

Visit ESR's Web site for more information, to visit its Online Teacher Center, or to sign up for its free monthly enewsletter.

You can contact ESR at:
Educators for Social Responsibility
23 Garden Street
Cambridge, MA 02138
1-800-370-2515
www.esrnational.org
educators@esrnational.org

About Youth Communication

Located in New York City, Youth Communication is a nonprofit youth development program whose mission is to teach writing, journalism, and leadership skills. The teenagers trained by Youth Communication, most of whom are New York City public high school students, become writers for two teen-written magazines, *New Youth Connections*, a general-interest youth magazine, and *Represent*, a magazine by and for young people in foster care. The stories in this anthology were originally published in these two magazines.

Youth Communication was created in 1980 in response to a nationwide study that found that the high school press was characterized by censorship, mediocrity, and racial exclusion. Keith Hefner cofounded the program and has directed it ever since.

Each year, more than 100 young people participate in Youth Communication's school-year and summer journalism workshops. They come from every corner of New York City, and the vast majority are African-American, Latino, or Asian teens. The teen staff members work under the direction of several full-time adult editors in Youth Communication's Manhattan newsroom.

Teachers, counselors, social workers, and other adults circulate the magazines to young people in their classes, after-school youth programs, and agencies. They distribute 70,000 copies of *New Youth Connections* each month during the school year, and 10,000 bimonthly copies of *Represent*. Teachers frequently tell the Youth Communication staff that teens in their classes—including students who are ordinarily resistant to reading—clamor for these publications. For the teen writers, the opportunity to reach their peers with important self-help information, and with accurate portrayals of their lives, motivates them to create powerful stories.

Running a strong youth-development program, while simultaneously producing quality teen magazines, requires a balance between a process that is sensitive to the complicated lives and emotions of the teen participants and one that is intellectually rigorous. That balance is sustained in the writing/teaching/editing relationship, which is the core of Youth Communication's program.

The teaching and editorial process begins with discussions between the adult editors and the teen staff, during which they seek to discover the stories that are both most important to each teen writer and potentially most appealing to the magazines' readers.

Once topics have been chosen, students begin the process of crafting their stories. For a personal story, that means revisiting events from the past to understand their significance for the future. For a commentary, it means developing a logical and persuasive argument. For a reported story, it means gathering information through research and interviews. Students look inward and outward as they try to make sense of their experiences and the world around them, and to find the points of intersection between personal and social concerns. That process can take a few weeks or a few months. Stories frequently go through four, five, or more drafts as students work on them under the guidance of editors in the same way that any professional writer does.

Many of the students who walk through Youth Communication's doors have uneven skills as a result of poor education, living under extremely stressful conditions, or coming from homes where English is a second language. Yet, to complete their stories, students must successfully perform a wide range of activities, including writing and rewriting, reading, discussion, reflection, research, interviewing, and typing. They must work as members of a team, and they must accept a great deal of individual responsibility. They learn to read subway maps, verify facts, and cope with rejection. They engage in explorations of truthfulness and fairness. They meet deadlines. They must develop the boldness to believe that they have something important to say, and the humility to recognize that saying it well is not a process of instant gratification, but usually requires a long, hard struggle through many discussions and much rewriting.

It would be impossible to teach these skills and dispositions as separate, disconnected topics such as grammar, ethics, or assertiveness training. However, the staff has found that students make rapid progress when they are learning skills in the context of an inquiry that is personally significant to them, and that they think will benefit their peers.

Writers usually participate in the program for one semester, though some stay much longer. Years later, many of them report that working at Youth Communication was a turning point in their lives—that it helped them acquire the confidence and skills they needed for success in their subsequent education and careers. Scores of Youth Communication's graduates have overcome tremendous obstacles to become journalists, writers, and novelists. Hundreds more are working in law, education, business, and other careers.

You can contact Youth Communication at:
Youth Communication
224 West 29th Street
New York, NY 10001
212-279-0708
www.youthcomm.org
info@youthcomm.org

Index

O

P

R

S

About the Authors

Al Desetta, M.A., is the editor of numerous books for young adults, including *The Struggle to Be Strong: True Stories by Teens About Overcoming Tough Times* (Free Spirit Publishing, 2001) and *The Heart Knows Something Different: Teenage Voices from the Foster Care System* (Persea Books, 1996). He is an editor at Youth Communication, a youth development organization in New York that teaches writing, journalism, and leadership skills to teens. He has served as instructor in the program's juvenile prison writing project; as editor of the organization's general interest teen magazine, *New Youth Connections;* and as founding editor of *Represent,* a nationwide magazine written by young people in foster care. Under his leadership, *Represent* received journalism awards from the Child Welfare League of America and the Casey Journalism Center for Children and Families. During the 1990–91 academic year, Desetta was a Charles H. Revson Fellow at Columbia University. He lives in upstate New York.

Sherrie Gammage, M.Ed., senior program associate with Educators for Social Responsibility, was the site coordinator for the Resolving Conflict Creatively Program in New Orleans, Louisiana, for six years. As an educator committed to anti-biased education, she works with local, regional, and national groups to create inclusive, just, and respectful learning environments in schools and community organizations. In 1999, as an ESR consultant, she facilitated a series of workshops in Tel Aviv, Israel, to teach conflict resolution to Israeli, Palestinian, and Arab educators and students. With Heather Coulehan, she is coauthor of *Countering Bullying and Harassment: A Facilitator's Guide to an Effective Peer Education Program in Middle and High Schools* (Educators for Social Responsibility, 2006). Gammage is a member of the adjunct faculty at the Lesley University Graduate School of Education, in both the Peaceable Schools and Literacy in Education programs. A former foster parent, she lives in New Orleans.

Other Great Books from Free Spirit

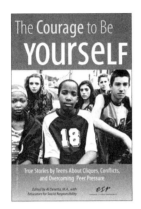

The Courage to Be Yourself
edited by Al Desetta, M.A., with Educators for Social Responsibility
Cassandra is hassled by her friends for sitting with the "wrong" kids at lunch. Jennifer gets harassed because she's overweight. Dwan's own family taunts her for not being "black enough." Yen is teased for being Chinese; Jamel for not smoking marijuana. Yet all find the strength to face their conflicts and the courage to be themselves. In 26 first-person stories, real teens write about their lives with searing honesty. They will inspire young readers to reflect on their own lives, work through their problems, and learn who they really are. For ages 13 & up.
$13.95, 160 pp.; softcover; 6" x 9"

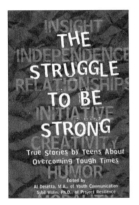

The Struggle to Be Strong
True Stories by Teens About Overcoming Tough Times
edited by Al Desetta, M.A., of Youth Communication, and Sybil Wolin, Ph.D., of Project Resilience
In 30 first-person accounts, teens tell how they overcame major life obstacles. As teens read this book, they will discover they're not alone in facing life's difficulties. They'll also learn about seven resiliencies—insight, independence, relationships, initiative, creativity, humor, and morality—that everyone needs to overcome tough times. For ages 13 & up.
$14.95; 192 pp.; softcover; illus.; 6" x 9"

A Leader's Guide to The Struggle to Be Strong
by Sybil Wolin, Ph.D., of Project Resilience, and Al Desetta, M.A., and Keith Hefner of Youth Communication
Activities, exercises, and questions invite teens to go deeper into the stories, relate them to their lives, recognize their potential for resilience, and start building resiliency skills. For teachers, social workers, case workers, clinicians, prevention specialists, counselors, and other adults who work with youth in grades 7–12.
$21.95; 176 pp.; softcover; 8½" x 11"

The Complete Guide to Service Learning
The Complete Guide to Service Learning
by Cathryn Berger Kaye, M.A.
A treasury of activities, ideas, quotes, reflections, resources, hundreds of annotated "Bookshelf" recommendations, and author interviews, presented within a curricular context and organized by theme. This eloquent, exhilarating guide can help teachers and youth workers engage young hearts and minds in reaching out and giving back. For teachers, grades K–12.
$29.95; 240 pp.; softcover; Otabind lay-flat binding; 8½" x 11"

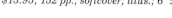

More Than a Label

Why What You Wear or Who You're With Doesn't Define Who You Are

by Aisha Muharrar

Preppie. Techie. Geek. Freak. Goth. Jock. These are just a few of the labels teens endure every day. Written by a teen, this book empowers students to stand up for themselves, understand others, and consider how labels define, limit, stereotype, and hurt. The book goes beyond labels to consider related issues—including cliques, peer pressure, popularity, racism, self-esteem, sexism, and homophobia. For ages 13 & up.

$13.95; 152 pp.; softcover; illus.; 6" x 9"

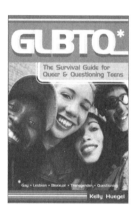

GLBTQ*

The Survival Guide for Queer & Questioning Teens

*Gay, Lesbian, Bisexual, Transgender, Questioning

by Kelly Huegel

A helpful look at the challenges and issues gay, lesbian, bisexual, transgendered, and questioning teens face at school, at home, and with friends. Recommended for any GLBTQ teen—and for any straight friend, parent, teacher, or other adult who cares and wants to understand. For ages 13 & up.

$15.95; 240 pp.; softcover; 6" x 9"

Respect

A Girl's Guide to Getting Respect & Dealing When Your Line Is Crossed

by Courtney Macavinta and Andrea Vander Pluym

This smart, savvy book helps teen girls get respect and hold on to it no matter what. It covers topics they deal with daily, like body image, family, friends, the media, school, relationships, and rumors. Girls learn that respect is always within reach because it starts on the inside. For ages 13 & up.

$15.95; 240 pp.; softcover; two-color illus., 7" x 9"

When Nothing Matters Anymore

A Survival Guide for Depressed Teens

by Bev Cobain, R.N.,C.

Written for teens with depression—and those who feel despondent, dejected, or alone—this powerful book offers help, hope, and potentially life-saving facts and advice. Includes true stories from teens who have dealt with depression, survival tips, resources, and more. For ages 13 & up.

$13.95; 176 pp.; softcover; illus.; 6" x 9"